# HEAR
# OUR PRAYER

BOOKS BY ROY PEARSON

The Hard Commands of Jesus
Here's a Faith for You
The Ministry of Preaching
Seeking and Finding God
This Do—and Live
Hear Our Prayer

# HEAR
# OUR PRAYER

*Prayers for Public Worship*

## Roy Pearson

McGRAW-HILL BOOK COMPANY, INC.

*New York · Toronto · London*

HEAR OUR PRAYER

Library of Congress Catalog Card Number: 60-53351

First Edition

49035

For

who, being laymen,
are yet ministers

# PREFACE

The warrant for a book of prayers for public worship is not that similar books do not already exist. As a parish minister, I always had a score or more of such volumes on a shelf by my desk, and I used them frequently. There is no substitute for the collections of classic prayers which are readily available, and the amount of the less historic literature of devotion is daily increasing.

But prayer—even that of corporate worship—is intensely personal; ministers differ widely in the ways they choose to lead their people to God; and congregations are incredibly diverse in their needs. However many books of prayers I had within reach during my ministry, I never seemed to have enough. This accounts in part for the prayers offered here, and it is the purpose of this book both to supplement the collections that the minister already possesses and to stimulate him to make his own contribution to the common store.

How can one acknowledge his indebtedness in such an undertaking? The words of the Bible itself can be neither escaped nor specifically designated in quotation, and some of the phrases that come to mind in composition almost certainly belong to prayers heard long ago and now wholly forgotten, with the exception of the single group of words too memorable to be lost. But with these exceptions, known or recognized, the prayers of this book are all new.

The choice of prayers for special occasions is necessarily arbitrary and intentionally limited. Some have reference to the church year and others to special days commonly recognized as having more or less religious significance, and there is a section on the sacraments and ordinances. But the bulk of the book is devoted to the long, hard pull of the "regular" services, and the prayers for unusual days are confined to areas that most ministers find unavoidable.

Some of the prayers will be found most suitable for reading by the pastor while the congregation listens, and others are equally adapted to individual or corporate use. In general, however, the book is meant less for reading in private than for speaking in public, and if the prayers are to have their full effectiveness, the leader will need to give attention not only to their meaning for the mind but also to their sound in the ear. Whatever else they may be, they are not a substitute for praying but an aid to one who prays.

# CONTENTS

# CONTENTS

CONTENTS

CONTENTS

# INTRODUCTION

When I was a parish minister, I often wondered why my people came to church. Sometimes as I sat in the chancel, I even wished that I might put the question directly to them and wait for an answer.

"Why didn't you stay at home this morning?" I wanted to ask. "Why aren't you out mowing your lawn or lying asleep in bed? What was it that kept you home from the picnic, or pulled you away from your television set, or told you not to wash your car? Did your wife drag you to church? Did your mother tell you that she had the hairbrush ready? Were you ushering today and hence compelled to be here although you longed to be somewhere else? Did your conscience steal around behind you, catch you unprepared, and leave you feeling that, for reasons which you could not clearly formulate, it was probably your duty to sit through a service again?"

Jesus once said that where two or three were gathered together in his name, he was in the midst of them, but if the truth were spoken, many people would be forced to say that they had never seen him in the public worship of their churches. Over and over again, in all parts of the land and in large parts of the world, groups of people come together in the name of Jesus, but if Jesus himself is actually present, they are not aware of it.

Some years ago, I read about a tall and talented gentleman who suddenly appeared in a little western town to prepare for the coming of a circus. He got the Boy Scouts to sponsor the affair. The local hotel saved twenty rooms for circus officials. A grocery store ordered a hundred pounds of frankfurters. The Coca-Cola Company delivered dozens of cases of its product. A truckload of hay was dumped on the green to feed the elephants. The tall and talented gentleman himself sold two hundred and fifty dollars worth of advertising for the circus program, and while he was working at it, the hotel donated his room, a restaurant supplied his board, and two doctors who treated him got free passes to the show as their fees for their services. Then the man left town. But the circus never came, and the grocer with the hundred pounds of frankfurters voiced the town's opinion. "That guy sure could talk!" he said.

That is the verdict that many people pass on the church. It sure can talk, but that often seems to be all it can do. Some criticism of the church is obviously wide of the mark, but those who love the church most would be among the first to admit that many churches do not have the goods they advertise. Jesus simply is

2

not in their midst, and neither is God; and when we really stop to think about it, we seldom find their absence strange. It is probably no secret among the angels that God is less than pleased with what happens in some of the churches that claim allegiance to him, and that he often has to use all of his restraint to keep from sticking hatpins into some of us, pouring cold water over our heads, or giving us a kind of heavenly "hotfoot." It is probably no secret that he fully understands what Jesus meant in saying that publicans and harlots would enter his kingdom before some of the "saints."

In 1751 William Warburton was Bishop of Gloucester, and on June 13 he sent to a friend a forthright letter about his faith in the church. "The church, like the Ark of Noah, is worth saving," he wrote, "not for the sake of the unclean beasts and vermin that almost filled it, and probably made most noise and clamor in it, but for the little corner of rationality, that was as much distressed by the stink within as by the tempest without."

It does not always happen, this undefined event that gives significance to public worship. Jesus is not always in the midst of those who say that they have come together in his name, and the lovers of the church would be less than candid if they refused to admit that the church's worship is frequently no more than a farce.

But God be praised that this is not the whole of the story. Jesus is still to be found precisely where he said that men would find him.

3

One summer night in London, my wife and I wandered down to Hyde Park. There was a crowd in the park that night, and everywhere we looked, we saw men perched on top of stepladders, shouting about something that they considered important. There were Communists, Catholics, Negroes, Protestant fundamentalists, Mormons, and one exhibitionist who apparently just wanted to talk and had no preference about his subject. But off to one side there was a group of people singing. They were natives of Wales, we were told, who, being in London, gathered in the park to sing the hymns they had learned at home. No one seemed to know where they lived, or who their leader was, or how they knew when their friends would be on hand to sing with them; but there they often were, and always singing. There were young people among them, and old people. Some were well dressed, and others still wore the clothes of the factories from which they had come. There were men, and there were women, and every now and then we saw a soldier or a sailor. But most important of all, these were happy people, triumphant people. As they threw back their heads and sang from full throats the beloved melodies of the Welsh hills, we saw that they were not posturing. We saw that they were unconscious of themselves. We saw that they had really met together in their Master's name, and with a sudden catching of our breath we knew that he of whom they sang was in their midst.

The presence that disturbed Wordsworth with the joy of elevated thoughts is not confined to setting suns

4

and the round ocean, not to the living air and the blue sky, nor even to the mind of man. I have met it among the Welsh singers in London, and I have met it in the formal worship of a church. I cannot explain it, any more than I can explain how some of the food I eat becomes my brain, and some my blood, and some my bones. I cannot explain it, but I know it is true. Take two or three people; put them together in Jesus' name; and you always have one more person than when you started. Jesus himself is always there.

But if he is, how does it happen that so many people take part in the worship services of the church with no consciousness of any presence other than their own? Why do their prayers seem so often unanswered? Why have they never met the living God?

Sometimes the explanation is simply that they have been looking for God in the wrong place. They have tried to find him where he cannot be found. A few years ago Dr. Nels F. S. Ferré was speaking about the sense in which God is present in the world. We think that God is everywhere, he said, and we claim that he is equally alive in all of the world. But that is not strictly true; for if it were, our human freedom would be nothing but illusion. In the impersonal sense that his power undergirds all things, God is truly present everywhere; but in the personal sense that his conscious being reaches out to touch our own, God deliberately absents himself in order that we can have liberty even from him. It is God's preference not to come where he is not wanted, not to enter where he is not asked.

When some lonely soul lifts up his heart in earnest prayer, God surely hears and answers; but the trouble with the common statement that you can worship God anywhere is that the most important parts of God's being are not to be found everywhere. All of God that we are likely to find in the places where many people proudly claim that they can worship him is a footprint, a part of his handiwork, a vague life force more akin to the wind than to the human soul.

Protestants have often been too sentimental about God, too unrealistic, too smug. We absent ourselves from public worship for reasons running all the way from rain, through the presence of week-end guests in the home or the lawn's need of mowing and the garden's need of weeding, to weariness after the party, the baby's feeding schedule, and the difficulty of preparing dinner if we go to church. But it all boils down to the truth, which is that we do not understand God's ways with men. Regular participation in the church's worship is more important than some of us have thought. The church is God's house, and if that means anything, it means that people are more likely to find God there than on a golf course belonging to the Pleasant Hills Country Club.

Sometimes, however, the reason why we do not find the presence in our midst is that we are making the wrong kind of effort. "Some people in church," writes W. R. Maltbie, "look like guests at a royal banquet who couldn't afford to be left out, but have been forbidden by their doctor to eat anything." So much of the church's "worship" is not really worship. So many of us do not really pray in our services, do not listen to the Scripture with any actual conviction that God is trying to speak to us through the words being read, do not sing the Gloria Patri with any significant awareness of God's majesty or the Doxology with any more attention than we give to saying, "Thank you," to the one who passes us the butter at the dinner table.

Everybody remembers the words of Jesus when he said, "Ask, and it shall be given you. Seek, and ye shall find. Knock, and it shall be opened unto you." Our usual emphasis is on the second part of each sentence: we shall be given, we shall find, the door will be opened. But that is the wrong place at which to start. We ought to begin where Jesus began: with the asking, with the seeking, with the knocking. The heavenly Father knows what we want before we ask it of him; but in the realms of the spirit, the giving often cannot come before the asking, and God cannot make some of his gifts available to us until we have prepared ourselves to receive them. The untrained ear cannot comprehend the intricacies of great music. The uninformed mind will not probe the depths of masterful poetry. And the arrogant soul cannot receive forgiveness. It is one thing to say to God that you want to feel his living presence in your heart. That is good, but it is not enough, any more than it is enough to say that you want to be an expert lawyer. That, too, may be good, but that, too, is not enough. There is discipline involved. There are study, work, humility, and faithfulness.

But the biggest reason why we do not feel the presence in our midst is probably that we have not done the will of him whom we say we wish to see. "Not everyone that saith unto me, Lord, Lord, shall enter the kingdom of heaven," Jesus warned, "but he that doeth the will of my Father which is in heaven." And who of us can claim that he has done the Father's will, followed his commandments exactly, pushed the matter past the point where embarrassment or hardship begins?

*Time* once cited as its "Headline of the Week" the following item from a newspaper in Pennsylvania: "SAFETY MAJOR ISSUE OF SAFETY COUNCIL." Such singlemindedness ought to be found in the church: Christianity ought to be the major issue of Christians. But often it is not. Making money takes precedence. Keeping up appearances has priority. Fear of ridicule comes first. To be gathered together in Jesus' name means to be gathered together in honesty, in earnestness, in the readiness to sacrifice oneself, in the willingness to take up a cross and go a second mile; and failing so to be gathered together, we can scarcely be surprised when we do not find the promised presence.

In one of my parsonages the heating was by steam. In the basement we had a conventional furnace, and from it the pipes ran up to the various rooms of the house, in each of which there was a radiator. We had thought that each room would be equally warm, but we soon discovered something strange about our heating system. Whenever we shut the door of a room, thus isolating it from the rest of the house, that room got cold. The radiator was still there and the heat was still on, but it made no difference. The room got cold.

Corporate worship is more important than many people have thought, more significant in the understanding of God, more surely essential to Christian growth. When we try to find the presence by ourselves, we usually become cold. It is when the doors are open that the warmth comes in. It is when we are gathered together in Jesus' name that his living spirit breathes upon our hearts, and cleanses our minds, and brings peace to our souls.

# PRAYERS
# IN THE VESTRY

We have gathered here, our Father, in the will to be thy ministers and to lead this people in thy worship. Fill our minds and our hearts with thy glory, we pray, and so transform us by thy power that we may become the means whereby this congregation finds its way to thee. Through Jesus Christ our Lord. *Amen.*

O thou who hast been man's dwelling place in all generations, we pray that thou thyself wilt dwell a while within this temple which men have made with their hands. Let the hour that lies ahead of us be rich in hope for those who wait to worship thee, and grant that those of us whose task it is to be their leaders lead them into knowledge of thy love and dedication to thy will. Through Jesus Christ our Lord. *Amen.*

Incline thine ear to us in this hour, O Lord. Hear thou the songs of our praise, and hearken thou to the voice of our supplication. In the worship of this congregation, vouchsafe that we may be a help and not a hindrance. Looking toward us, may these people look through us, and seeing us, even more surely see thee. In Jesus' name. *Amen.*

Almighty and eternal God, whose glory heaven and earth proclaim, help us so to lift up our voices in praise and so to speak thy word in truth, that those who have come to thy house to worship may leave it to serve. Through Jesus Christ our Lord. *Amen.*

Loving and compassionate Father, who carest for all of thy children with a kindness passing our knowledge, open our hearts to the needs of this congregation waiting now for us to lead it in its worship. If there be joys which have not recognized their origin in thee, if there be sorrows still untouched by thy grace, if there be sins unforgiven or pains unassuaged or hopes unfulfilled—let us not be careless of their presence in our midst; and through some ministry of mind or body, through some helpfulness of anthem or sermon, through some leadership in hymn or prayer—grant that we may be the heralds of thy gospel and the bearers of thy saving power. Through Jesus Christ our Lord. *Amen.*

We give thanks to thee, O God. We give thanks, and remembering all they lovingkindness to us, we offer thee this ministry of song and spoken word. Through our frailty speak thou to this congregation with strength; through our ignorance speak thou to it in truth; and through our sin let thy pure love so descend upon these men and women that they may find in this hour the light and peace which come from none but thee. Through Jesus Christ our Lord. *Amen.*

God of the ages and Father of men, who art thyself a laborer and who dost ask of man no service which thou hast not long since performed thyself, through the week that is past we have sought to further thy will in daily work and fellowship. As we come to thy house this day, we seek to serve thee by lifting up the hearts of this people in their prayer and praise, and we ask that accepting us as the humble agents of thy purpose, thou wilt keep us from bearing false witness to thine intent for this congregation. Through Jesus Christ our Lord. *Amen.*

When we sing, O Lord, help us to sing thy praise. When we speak, stir us to speak thy word. Leading us now into worship, lead us also into such awareness of thy majesty and tenderness that even through the imperfections which make us unworthy to be thy ministers, thy perfect holiness may shine upon this congregation. Through Jesus Christ our Lord. *Amen.*

Where we would have this congregation go, our Father, we pray that thou wilt cause us to go before them. If we would have this people enter thy house in quietness, quiet first our own minds. If we would have

*13*

them look to thee in eager faith, open first our own hearts to thy coming. If we would have them hear thy word and heed, make us first willing to hear and heed, ourselves. In Jesus' name. *Amen.*

O thou who dwellest both in heaven and on earth, and who didst love the world enough to send it thy Son, we draw ourselves apart from the clamorous tasks of the passing day, and we lay this hour on thine altar as a gift for none but thee. Use us as thou wilt, we pray, and so multiply our little ministry in thy name that thy strength may be made perfect in our weakness. Through Jesus Christ our Lord. *Amen.*

Forgive us the sins, O Lord, which could so easily turn to vanity this service which we have prepared for thy praise. Chasten our minds of their evil; purge our souls of their wrong; and so cleanse our hearts of their iniquity that seeing thee ourselves, we may make plain thy ways to this people. Through Jesus Christ our Lord. *Amen.*

Again we have come to thy house to lead our friends and neighbors in worship, our Father, and again we pray that thou wilt do through us what we could never do alone. Chasten us that we may not stand in the way of thy will. Kindle us that we may speak thy word in boldness and sing thy praise in joy. And as we minister in thy name, may we minister with earnestness and wisdom. Through Jesus Christ our Lord. *Amen.*

*14*

Go with us in this service, Lord, that we may go with thee; and grant that they may go with thee also who wait for us to guide them in their praise. Through Jesus Christ our Lord. *Amen.*

Grant, our Father, that we may be a voice for those who have gathered here to worship thee. At organ bench or choir stall, at lectern or pulpit or altar, give us power so to sing and so to speak that prisoned hearts may gain release and that praising and confessing, asking and receiving, consecrating and rejoicing, this people may this day be born again, new creatures in thy sight. Through Jesus Christ our Lord. *Amen.*

We have come early to thy house, our Father, that we might better prepare ourselves to lead this congregation in its worship, and we pray that neither our waywardness of life nor our carelessness of manner may prove stumbling blocks to those to whom we seek to minister. Let the moment that still remains before we join our fellows be a moment spent so quietly with thee that we may be with thee in all of the moments beyond it. Through Jesus Christ our Lord. *Amen.*

We are not worthy of the task that lies ahead of us, our Father. We are not wise enough to lead our fellows into thy presence. We are not strong enough. We are not good enough. Yet thou dost use the common earth to nurture the rose, and thou dost transform the dust of the sky into the glory of the sunset. So we put ourselves into thy hands for this hour of worship, and we pray that if thou canst not make us the means of bringing this people to thee, thou wilt at least save us from being the means of keeping them away. Through Jesus Christ our Lord. *Amen.*

As we need thee ourselves, O Lord, we know that others need thee, too. Help us therefore both to seek thy presence for our own sakes and also to spare no effort which would bring our brothers to thy throne beside us. Through Jesus Christ our Lord. *Amen.*

Grant, Lord, that some word spoken, some song sung, or some deed done may bring the needed ministry to those who wait for us to lead them in thy praise. Through Jesus Christ our Lord. *Amen.*

# PRAYERS
# OF INVOCATION

## GENERAL PRAYERS

Almighty and eternal God, who dost ever come to meet thy people when they go in search of thee, come thou to us who gather here to praise thy name. Come thou in such quietness that only the silent will hear thee. Come thou in such lowliness that only the humble will discern thee. Come thou in such goodness that only the pure in heart will desire thee. But first make us silent; first make us humble; first make us pure in heart. Through Jesus Christ our Lord. *Amen.*

Grant, Lord, that thinking, we may think thy thoughts; that speaking, we may speak thy word; that singing, we may sing to thy praise; that hearing, we may hear thy truth; and that willing, we may make thy will our own, so that walking forth at the end of our worship, we may walk in thy love and thy peace, and departing from one another, not depart from thee. Through Jesus Christ our Lord. *Amen.*

O thou who art the Way and the Life, we thank thee that thou art also the Truth, and we pray that we who daily strive to walk the way and live the life may not be unaware of thee when thou dost come to us as truth. Keep us from forging thy name to prejudice and error. Save us from the indigestion of unassimilated information. Guard us against the anarchy of unrelated facts. And then cleanse our souls that we may be still in thy presence; open our minds that we may welcome news of thy glory; warm our hearts that they may rejoice in word of thy love. Through Jesus Christ our Lord. *Amen.*

Save us here, O Lord, from the tyranny of the tiny. Protect us from such fascination with the insignificant that we have no time to swing the heavy picks and axes of thy kingdom's building. But save us, too, from failing so frequently in little things that we fail at last in everything. Keep us from laughing so loud at the obvious that we do not understand when thou dost choose to make it the voice of thy will. Through Jesus Christ our Lord. *Amen.*

O thou whose eagerness to be found by thy creatures exceeds that of thy creatures to find, increase, we pray, the hunger of our hearts for thyself. Help us to put our other hopes aside and in these moments have no purpose but such knowledge of thee that we may discover who we really are and how thou dost intend that

*18*

we should serve thee on the earth. Make us quiet. Make us expectant. Make us willing. Through Jesus Christ our Lord. *Amen.*

Eternal God, revealed in Jesus Christ and ever through thy Holy Spirit in our midst today, we prod our minds in quest of surer sight of thee and of thy ways with that which thou hast made. Open our eyes, we pray thee. Quicken our hearts. And so thrust back our horizons that our understanding draws a little closer to thine own, and seeing life as thou dost see it, we move along our portion of it with neither harm to our fellows nor offense to thy will. Through Jesus Christ our Lord. *Amen.*

Almighty and eternal God, who didst of old reveal thyself to men and summon them to walk with thee in humble faith and love, we thank thee that thy trumpet calls across the hills today and that still the loyal hear and heed. Grant now that in these moments spent together here, our minds may be illumined, our hearts warmed, our bodies renewed and our souls so purified that seeing thee, we may both understand thy will and do it. Through Jesus Christ our Lord. *Amen.*

Eternal Lord, whose everlasting ways are goodness and whose never fainting will is peace and righteousness, we have gathered here with hearts both grateful and distraught. We praise thee for the wonder and beauty of the world which thou hast created, and we ask thy forgiveness for the havoc man has made of it. Be thou present in our midst this hour, and keep us conscious that thou art. And through some ministry now offered us, touch our hearts and heal our hurts; win our wills and cleanse our souls; and send us forth new creatures in thy sight and strong to walk where thou wouldst have us go. Through Jesus Christ our Lord. *Amen.*

O thou who, being homeless, art everywhere at home, and who, loving each of thy children as if he alone were thy child, yet lovest all of thy creatures as if thou hadst no special love for any one of them, tarry now among us here. Let our hearts awhile be home to thee, and help us so to respond to thy love that we may have the strength and will to work for peace and righteousness upon the earth. Guide us into humility. Lead us into quietness. Lure us into faith and trust in thee. Through Jesus Christ our Lord. *Amen.*

O thou who once didst brood upon the emptiness, and out of nothing bring forth the worlds, and on the earth give life to man, we pray that thou wilt continue thy creation in us. Being members of the church, we have gathered here as Christians: grant that departing, we may be more nearly Christlike. Spur us into eagerness to surrender ourselves in thy service. Lead us into readiness to die for our faith, and even more, to live for it. Through Jesus Christ our Lord. *Amen.*

God of all wisdom and knowledge, in whose eyes no sparrow falls unseen and in whose righteousness each act of man is measured in merciful justice, we seek thy face in confession of our sins and in need of thy pardon. Forgive, we pray, the wrongs that we have done both in blindness and in sight, and in our blindness give us vision, and in our seeing grant us the will to love the good that we have scorned. Through Jesus Christ our Lord. *Amen.*

Almighty and eternal God, beyond whom nothing is and in whom nothing lies unseen or uncontrolled, we praise thee for the infinite wonder of thy goodness to men. Thou lovest even the unlovable, and causing thy sun to rise on the just, thou dost not leave the unjust in darkness. From thee came life and all that brings us joy, and in sorrow and death we find in thee a refuge from our fears. Accept therefore these words that we speak to thy glory, and vouchsafe that we may prove our love for thee by serving those whom thou dost love. Through Jesus Christ our Lord. *Amen.*

Forgive us, our Father, for all that we have done amiss. For thoughts conceived in anger and nurtured in hatred, for words uttered in haste and called back in vain, for deeds undertaken in haughtiness and pursued in stubborn malice—forgive us as we bow before thee in this holy house. In these moments of our worship, take thy place among us, we pray, until made clean in

21

thy presence we stand forth new creatures in thy sight.
Through Jesus Christ our Lord. *Amen.*

From the harried world of the daily round we turn
aside to seek thy peace, O Lord—from the jungles of
competition with our fellows, from the swamps of tasks
that multiply beyond our power to manage them, from
the quicksands of temptations that swallow down our
good intentions. Push back with gentleness the doors we
leave ajar for thee, and in the quietness of this place
apart, bring calm to every restless soul. Lead us into
closer fellowship with thee; teach us the truths that
never change; and in thy never-failing power let our
weakness find fresh hope. Through Jesus Christ our
Lord. *Amen.*

Almighty and eternal God, whose wisdom never
slumbers and whose goodness never sleeps, save us from
such comfort in thy bounty that we never feel our fellows' pain. Where there is hunger or homelessness,
where there is cold or lack of friendship, where there is
strife or suffering or hatred—grant that our minds may
be led in this hour, and going forth at end of worship,
may we go with the knowledge and the will to be the
bearers of thy love. Through Jesus Christ our Lord.
*Amen.*

Almighty and eternal God, beyond whom nothing
is and without whom nothing is worthy to endure, save
us from the mouthing of words which have no meaning

in our lives. Keep our minds awake in this hour, we pray; let our hearts be warmed by thy love; and so fling wide the gates of our souls that thou who art everywhere outside us mayest henceforth rule and reign within us. Through Jesus Christ our Lord. *Amen.*

O thou eternal Father, whose power never fails, whose wisdom never falters, and whose love never grows weary, grant that in this time of worship our weakness may glorify thee, our folly praise thee, and our discord magnify thy holy name. Through all our imperfections continue thou in thy perfection, and by thy pure and healing grace thrust out of our hearts each sullied thought and unworthy affection. Through Jesus Christ our Lord. *Amen.*

Turn not away from our sin, O Lord, and cast us not aside in our blindness. As far as the heaven is from the earth, so far art thou removed from our transgressions. As the day is to the night, so is thy righteousness to our iniquity. But still we are thy children, and still we long to return to our Father's house. Save us, then, because of ourselves and in spite of ourselves, and as we come to thee in penitence and praise, spurn not our pledge that henceforth we shall be thy faithful servants. Through Jesus Christ our Lord. *Amen.*

We believe in thee, our Father. Help thou our unbelief, and if thou dost accept our offerings of faith, thrust not away the doubts that we bring to thy throne.

Satisfy our minds with thy truth in this hour; fill our hearts with thy peace; and so minister to our souls that going forth at the end of our worship, we shall know how to live with the unknowable. Through Jesus Christ our Lord. *Amen.*

Almighty and eternal God, whose thunder is in quietness and whose still, small voice speaks louder than the earthquake, the wind, or the fire, let thy whispers be shouts in our ears, we pray. Be not too patient with our deafness to thy word, and grant that our inattentiveness to thee may not become the road to our destruction. Waken us, and keep us awake. Open our eyes to see the hurts of men that twist thy heart in pain, and lead our hands to heal the hurts which thou hast made our eyes to see. Through Jesus Christ our Lord. *Amen.*

God of mystery and wonder, whose light is often brightest in the shadows and whose candles shine most surely when the darkness descends on the world, we turn to thee in a twilight which seems to hold more promise of the night than of the day. If we have sinned, we pray that thou wilt forgive us. If we are weary, we pray that thou wilt enliven us. If we are bewildered, we pray that thou wilt instruct us. And through all the dusk that shrouds the onward way, we ask that we may find in the face of Jesus Christ the light of the knowledge of thy glory. *Amen.*

Come thou to us, our Father. Come thou to us in this hour. From far or near, come thou to us that we may come to thee. Cleanse us in our wickedness. Straighten us in our crookedness. Renew us in our feebleness. Persuade us in our unwillingness. Through Jesus Christ our Lord. *Amen.*

Almighty and eternal God, whose love suffers long and whose patience turns not away from the prideful boasting of thy children, forgive, we pray, the arrogance by which we shut thee from our hearts. If we have said that we were self-made men and women, lead us into shame for what we have made of ourselves. Teach us how much of our sufficiency rests in none but thee, and so make us humble that being weak, we may yet be strong because thy mighty hand sustains us. Through Jesus Christ our Lord. *Amen.*

O thou who dost brood upon the patient silences and manifest thyself most clearly in the stillness that pleads for thy presence, let the quiet of this hour offer welcome to thy word. Be known, we pray, by those who would be known by thee. To them who listen, speak; to them who search, reveal; and to them who wait, come. In Jesus' name. *Amen.*

O thou whose blessing is on the man who walks not in the counsel of the wicked, nor stands in the way of sinners, nor sits in the seat of scoffers, but whose delight is in thy law and who meditates upon that law both day and night, grant us so to be that man that we may be like a tree planted by streams of water, that yields its fruit in its season and allows not its leaf to wither. And in all that we do in thy name, vouchsafe that we may prosper. Through Jesus Christ our Lord. *Amen.*

O thou whose name alone is exalted and whose glory exceeds both the earth and the heavens, have mercy on us in our sin. Put into our hearts a new desire to serve thee, and let not the evil we have done of old corrupt the good to which we pledge the days that wait for us to live them. Through Jesus Christ our Lord. *Amen.*

Almighty and everlasting God, at whose command the worlds were born and in whose image man was made, incline our hearts to understand thy will for all the people thou hast placed upon the earth. Save us from calling thee Lord while we seek to dethrone thee, and keep us from assuming that what we cannot comprehend we need not acknowledge. Through Jesus Christ our Lord. *Amen.*

O thou who makest all things new, renew in us the will to serve thee. If our hearts have grown cold, let them be warmed by thy nearness. If our eyes have become clouded, restore the sight that once they knew. If our courage has faltered and fallen, lift up our souls to face the world and have no fear. Through Jesus Christ our Lord. *Amen.*

We praise thee, O Lord. We praise thee in thy sanctuary; we praise thee in thy mighty firmament; we praise thee for thy mighty deeds; we praise thee according to thine exceeding greatness. Accept our praise, we beseech thee, and so direct our ways that confessing thee with our lips, we may not deny thee with our lives. Through Jesus Christ our Lord. *Amen.*

O thou who hast many foes, grant that we may be among thy friends. Let not our thirst to be approved by men precede our will to be approved by thee, and lead us in this hour so to put our trust in thee, that we acknowledge thee to be the Lord as willingly beneath the cross as by the empty tomb. In Jesus' name. *Amen.*

O thou who madest heaven and earth, the sea, and all that is in them, dwell here a moment now that we may dwell with thee. Let this hour be a threshold to thy presence, and in thy light may we see light. Through Jesus Christ our Lord. *Amen.*

Almighty and eternal God, who dost give ear to our words and hearken to the sound of our cry, let all who take refuge in thee rejoice. Let them ever sing for joy, and do thou defend them, that those who love thy name may exult in thee and those whom thou dost bless be covered with thy favor as with a shield. Through Jesus Christ our Lord. *Amen.*

God of grace and God of glory, who hast made the nations our heritage and the ends of the earth our possession, save us from so living that thou hast no choice but to break us with a rod of iron and dash us in pieces like a potter's wheel. Teach us to serve thee in awe and righteousness, lest thy wrath be kindled against us and thine anger rise up in our midst to destroy us. Through Jesus Christ our Lord. *Amen.*

Speak thou to us in this hour, Lord. As spirit makes itself known to spirit, speak to us, and help us to hear. Speak thou in wrath if they be here who flaunt thy light and lordship. Speak thou in peace if they be here whose hearts are torn by doubt and fear. Speak thou in summons sharp and loud if they be here who slumber through their brothers' pain. In Jesus' name. *Amen.*

Arise, O Lord. Lift up thy hand, and forget not the afflicted among us. Where there is sorrow or pain, where there is hatred or hardness of heart, where there is weakness or fear or need of any kind—there be thou in love that never fails and in righteousness unceasing; and vouchsafe that they who put their trust in thee may stand in thy prevailing might and by thy might prevail. In Jesus' name. *Amen.*

O thou who seemest often to stand afar off and to hide thyself in times of trouble, cleanse our hearts that we may see thee standing close beside us and revealing thyself most surely to those who seek thee most truly; and save us both from looking for thee where thou art not and from failing to find thee where thou art. Through Jesus Christ our Lord. *Amen.*

Guide us, our Father, that we may recognize thy voice whenever conscience summons us to courage, whenever helpfulness brings satisfaction and friendship points the way to joy. So lead us through the ruins of the age that is gone that we may approach the coming days with minds enlightened by the folly of the past, with hearts cleansed of their sin, and with souls warmed by thy love and aflame with thy will. Through Jesus Christ our Lord. *Amen.*

Almighty and eternal God, who lovest the poor in spirit, the meek, and those who mourn; whose favor rests with the merciful, the pure in heart, and those who hunger and thirst after righteousness; and who holdest in thy holy care the peacemakers and all who are persecuted and reviled for Jesus' sake: help us so to find our blessedness in doing thy will that we may rejoice and be glad all our days on the earth and receive at last that heavenly reward which belongs alone to those who have not sought it. Through Jesus Christ our Lord. *Amen.*

Teach us, our Father, to walk the narrow way between vaunting our faith on street corners and hiding our light under baskets. Save us from putting on fear the label of humility, from dressing laziness in the robes of meekness, and from seeking safety in burying the talents which were meant for the risk of investment. We would not become hypocrites by claiming greater faith than we have, but keep us also from becoming hypocrites by claiming less. We would not stand and pray in order that we may be seen of men, but protect us, too,

29

from never standing, never praying. Through Jesus Christ our Lord. *Amen.*

Save us, our Father, both from the worry which does no more than prove the smallness of our faith and from the peacefulness which tells the world that our eyes are closed, our ears stopped, and our consciences asleep. Let not our privilege become a curse in time of judgment, and dozing by the evening hearthstones, may we not be doing evil to our brother in the cold. We are Christians, Lord: make us Christlike. We are church members: make us disciples. In Jesus' name. *Amen.*

Righteous and gracious God, who art just in all thy ways and kind in all thy doings, be near us when we call on thee; hear us when we cry to thee; and save us in our need of thee. Let not our sin provoke thee to spurn us, and in joy or in sorrow, by peace or by pain, through life or through death, grant that we may not be separated from thy love. In Jesus' name. *Amen.*

Do with us as thou wilt, our Father. Be our peace if quietness can prove itself the herald of thy purpose. Be our pain if only agony can cut the blinding veils of pride. Through Jesus Christ our Lord. *Amen.*

Almighty God, who dost not change from age to endless age, help us so to rest on thee that we can truly rest. Take away the fears that make the ground beneath us seem to tremble. Steady us in knowing that the earth is but one province in thy kingdom, that time is but a segment of eternity, that birth and death are but the doors that lead from one room to another, and that thou hast forever for the shaping of the human soul. Through Jesus Christ our Lord. *Amen.*

Save us, our Father. Save us from ourselves. Save us in spite of ourselves. Storm the beachheads of our little worlds; invade the tiny islands of our self-sufficiency; and establish over us a sovereignty beyond dispute. For knowing thee in part, we know we need thee in much greater part; and needing thee, we wait for thee. Through Jesus Christ our Lord. *Amen.*

Open our hearts, O Lord, until thou canst do for us the good for which we cry but bar our doors against receiving. Give us pride as pride is the self-respect of those who understand the labor thou hast spent in their creation; but rob us of pride as pride is the arrogance of him who does not comprehend his absolute dependence on thy life and love. Teach us gratitude that thou hast given us a mind to probe the mysteries that crowd around the little light by which we see, and vouchsafe that we may use the skills of mind to serve and not to thwart thy will; but save us from such unreasonable use of our reason that we place upon it greater burdens than it has strength to bear and claim for it a larger competence than it can justify. If we have not goodness, deny us greatness. If we cannot be kind, keep us from calm. Make us restless till we find our rest in thee, and grant that we may know thee when we find thee. Through Jesus Christ our Lord. *Amen.*

Save us, our Father, from such eagerness for heaven that we shun the holy gift of earth. Keep us from so dwelling through hope in tomorrow that we never see the deeds that summon us today. Help us to know that thou art where thy people are; lead us to understand that with thee the great are the good; and then so strangle our lusts, and suffocate our prejudices, and batter down our jealousies that on the darkened ways of earthly life thy light may shine and not be dimmed. Through Jesus Christ our Lord. *Amen.*

We need thee, Lord. We need thy wisdom as we try to make the choices which we have no wit to make but still must wisely put behind us. We need thy strength for tasks that loom as mountains on the way but still must be removed if we would pass them by. We need thy mercy as we daily fashion noble resolutions and daily leave them bent and broken on the road. So we pray that thou wilt manifest thyself to us in this hour of worship and so be known and recognized and welcome that henceforth we may walk with thee in faith and faithfulness. Through Jesus Christ our Lord. *Amen.*

Almighty and everlasting God, whose light so shineth in the darkness that the darkness cannot put it out, we seek the life of those who need no light of the sun since thou dost illumine their way. There are so many dark corners in our lives—so many memories of evil we have done, so many thoughts to which we cannot turn without regret, so many fears and jealousies and hatreds. Shine in our hearts, we pray, and give us the light of the knowledge of thy glory in Jesus Christ our Lord. *Amen.*

Loving and compassionate Father, who didst send thy Son to give knowledge of salvation to thy people, save us from ourselves. Keep us from the fears that nurture arrogance and from the insecurity that fosters greed. Redeem us from contentment with the ordinary, satisfaction with the commonplace, and complacency in what imposes no demands upon us. Grant us such sureness of faith in life eternal that we are not crushed by living now, but yet so deep a confidence that life is good today, that every moment is a song of praise that we can be alive. Through Jesus Christ our Lord. *Amen.*

O thou whose glory the heavens declare and whose handiwork the firmament showeth, help us to hear thy word as day unto day uttereth speech and night unto night showeth knowledge. Bless us with understanding of our errors, and cleanse us from our secret faults. Keep back thy servants from presumptuous sins, and let the words of our mouths and the meditations of our hearts be acceptable in thy sight, O Lord, our strength and our redeemer. *Amen.*

33

Eternal Spirit, who art nigh unto all them that call upon thee, to all that call upon thee in truth, fulfill now the desire of them that fear thee. Hear their cry, and save them. For thou art gracious and full of compassion, slow to anger and great in thy mercy. *Amen.*

# SPECIAL OCCASIONS

## *Advent and Christmas*

O thou whose advent was proclaimed of old by seer and by prophet, and who didst come at last in ways that neither prophet knew nor seer saw, keep us alert to the signs of thy coming today. Open our minds, warm our hearts, cleanse our souls, and give our bodies strength to bear the sudden burdens of thy need; and shouldst thou choose again a stable as thy gateway to the world, grant that we may not be blind to thy glory or deaf to thy word. Through Jesus Christ our Lord. *Amen.*

Almighty and eternal God, who didst send thy Son to preach good news to the poor, to proclaim release to the captives and recovering of sight to the blind, to set at liberty those who are oppressed, and to proclaim the acceptable year of the Lord, we praise thee that the Scriptures have been fulfilled in our ears. For all thy ministry through him we give thee eager thanks, and as the day draws near when we shall hail his birth anew, we pray that ready for the manger, we may be as ready for the cross. In Jesus' name. *Amen.*

Blessed art thou, O God, for thou hast visited and redeemed thy people, and hast raised up a horn of salvation for us in the house of thy servant David. We praise thee for the prophets of old who have heralded the coming of thy Son to give knowledge of salvation to his people in the forgiveness of their sins, to bring light to those who sit in darkness and in the shadow of death, and to guide our feet into the way of peace. Vouchsafe, we pray, that what thy prophets have foretold we may prepare our hearts to receive. Through Jesus Christ our Lord. *Amen.*

We magnify thy name, O Lord, and we rejoice in thy salvation. Thou hast shown strength with thine arm and scattered the proud in the imagination of their hearts. Thou hast put down the mighty from their thrones and exalted those of low degree. Thou hast filled the hungry with good things, and the rich thou hast sent empty away. In remembrance of thy mercy help thy servants now, we pray, and as thou hast spoken to our fathers, speak here to their children. Through Jesus Christ our Lord. *Amen.*

1158537

Almighty and eternal God, who so loved the world that thou didst give thine only Son, that whoever believes in him should not perish but have eternal life, we have come to thy house to praise thee for a gift too great for human praise. In vain we strive to speak the gratitude which still remains unspeakable, and with the heavenly hosts of Bethlehem we sing again the ancient song, praying that glory be thine in the highest, and on earth peace among men with whom thou art pleased. Through Jesus Christ our Lord. *Amen.*

Let not thy star grow dim above the manger, Lord. The world is too much with us day by day, and in the night we need to know that thou dost still support the meek against the mighty. Recall us therefore from the distant lands where we have sought a kingdom of our own, and grant that finding thine within the stable, we may not be blind to what we see. Through Jesus Christ our Lord. *Amen.*

## New Year's Day

Almighty and eternal God, whose love never faileth and changeth not from age to endless age, we thank thee that the old year slips so speedily behind us, that memories grow dim and our foolishness is forgotten, that wounds are healed and our strength is restored. Forgive, we pray, the sins no stream of time can wash away, the hurts whose scars remain unsmoothed, the dreams that died and have no hope of resurrection; but have no patience with us if the new year finds us living still within the old. We have only one back: help us to turn it toward the past. We have but one face: teach us to point it gladly toward the days unborn. Through Jesus Christ our Lord. *Amen.*

O thou who didst beget us in body, beget us once again in spirit. Let not the old year chain us to its sorrows nor make its little joys a ceiling shutting out thy mighty sun. Put mountains on our pathways, Lord, and give us faith enough to move them. Lay heavy burdens on our shoulders, and grant us strength enough to carry them. And through the turning seasons, turn us ever toward thy face. Through Jesus Christ our Lord. *Amen.*

## *Epiphany*

O thou whose glory fills the heavens, let it fill the earth. Bless not those who claim thee for themselves alone, nor grant success to any word of thee which is not a word for all the world. Send out thy light and thy truth. Let them lead us, and if they take us to thy holy hill, permit us no contentment on the heights unless our brothers stand beside us. Through Jesus Christ our Lord. *Amen.*

Almighty and eternal God, who willest that all thy children be disciples of thy Son, give us the will to exercise our own discipleship. If thou hast called us out of darkness into light, make us restless while our brothers dwell in darkness; and as thou didst reveal thyself of

*37*

old to those who were not of thy people, reveal thyself anew to those who know thee not. Let the nations praise thee. Let all the nations praise thee. Through Jesus Christ our Lord. *Amen.*

O thou who didst not rest content when convenient shepherds knelt before the manger, and who didst cause thy star to shine on kings in realms afar, ordain, we pray, that all the kingdoms of the world become the kingdom of thy Son. Teach us to sing the Lord's song in the strange lands of business and science, of literature and art, of peoples that have never heard thy name and nations that have judged thee by the enemies they thought to be thy friends. Refute the prejudice that makes us hate our brothers; upset the selfishness that blinds us to the debt we owe thy heavy-laden children; disturb the lethargy that keeps us from thy service; and stabbing us awake, redeem us from the sleep of death. In Jesus' name. *Amen.*

## Race Relations Sunday

Father of light, make us blind. Seal our sight against the different colors of thy creatures, the varied shapes of eye and nose, the sundered ways with food and clothing. School us to see as thou dost see, to look not on the outward appearance but only on the heart; and when at last our eyes again are opened, grant that we may praise thee for the glad dissimilarities of thy creation. Through Jesus Christ our Lord. *Amen.*

God of love, save us from hating thee. We say that we love thee, but how can we love the Creator when we hate his creatures? We affirm that thou hast made man in thine own image, but how can we exalt the Father if we loathe the child? Guide us therefore lest renouncing our brother, we disown our Father, or seeking our Father, fail to look for him beside our brother. In Jesus' name. *Amen.*

Art thou white or black, our Father? Dost thou belong to east or west, to north or south? Are thine eyes straight or slanted? Is thy nose long or short, thy hair dark or light, thy lips thick or thin? Save us, we pray, from trying to create thee in our own image, reduce thee to our own level, confine thee within our own limits; and vouchsafe that beholding the wonderful diversity of thy creatures, we may find its origin in thee, who, creating all, lovest all that thou createst. Through Jesus Christ our Lord. *Amen.*

## Ash Wednesday

Almighty and eternal God, who didst create the world and see that it was good, forgive us that we have turned thy gardens into deserts. We kneel in penitence before thee as we call to mind the hatred that has thwarted the healing shadows of thy peace, the greed that has devoured the cooling rivers of thy mercy, and the envy that has scorched the fair fields of thy love. Scorn not thy children as they seek thy pardon, and grant that, lonely in the wilderness which we ourselves have made, we may find again beside us him who knew a wilderness before us, Jesus Christ, our Lord. *Amen.*

We have sinned, our Father. We have sinned against thee, and we are no more worthy to be called thy children. We have fled from the homeland, dwelt in the far country, wasted our substance in living unworthy to be called life, and, destined for the bread of heaven, hungered even for the husks of hell. Have mercy on us, we beseech thee, and giving us what we have no right even to ask, lead us to commit to thee the faithfulness which thou hast the right to expect without asking. Through Jesus Christ our Lord. *Amen.*

O thou who longest only that thy people find in thee the love that leads to love of one another, let not this time be days of inactivity, postponement, and delay. Save us from the sins of evil done, but save us also from the sins of righteousness withheld. Drive us often into silence, but from the silence lure us no less often into service. Chasten us that we may know our sin, but enlighten us that we may not neglect our hope. Keep us busy, and let our business always be our Father's. Through Jesus Christ our Lord. *Amen.*

## Palm Sunday

Almighty King and merciful Father, who understandest both the cowardice of the reckless and the courage of the fearful, we praise thee for him who had known too much of man to be fearless but who had lived too long with thee to be unfaithful. Hosanna to the Son of David! Blessed be he who steadfastly set his face toward Jerusalem and, riding on a beast of burden, took upon himself the burdens of the world. Hosanna! Hosanna in the highest! *Amen.*

O thou whose Jerusalems are as many as man's sins and whose crosses as timeless as time, behold, the Master rides again to Zion, and again the multitudes surround him in his glory. Let our praise be as branches of palm, we pray thee, and our prayers like garments spread on the road; and grant that we may stand no closer to him when the crowds cry "Hosanna!" than when the shout has turned to "Crucify!" *Amen.*

Forgive us, Lord, that we are so unstable, that there is such a little space between our loyalties and our desertions, that the lips which cry "Hosanna!" can so quickly clamor "Crucify!" We bless thee for the Master's hour of triumph, when the crowds spread their garments before him and followed with their branches of palm; but we bow in shame as we recall that other day so soon to come, when the cross was raised at Calvary, and men of hatred killed the man of love. Number us, we pray, among the multitudes that hail the King in his glory, but keep us not apart from those who stand beside him in his lonely pain. *Amen.*

*41*

## Maundy Thursday

Merciful Father, who dost never bring pain to thy children without pain to thyself, spare us not the suffering that faithfulness demands. If it be possible, let the cup of agony pass from our lips, but if the maladies of earth are now too strong for cups with sweeter waters, if the needs of men have grown too grim for ways with fairer skies, if truth and righteousness have been too long repressed for wars with easy victories—give us courage for the death that ends in life. Thy will be done, O Lord. Thy will be done—in us. In Jesus' name. *Amen.*

O thou who dost never slumber, never sleep, share thy wakefulness with thy children. Save us from the fevered restlessness of those who have no knowledge of thy power, but let not our heads lie undisturbed on our pillows while thou dost stalk the haunts of wretchedness around us. We do not deserve our peace; we do not deserve our safety; we do not deserve our comfort. Spare us then the shame that we could not even watch with thee while thou didst seek an answer to the pain of thy people, and keep us awake, lest sleeping, we sleep the sleep of death. Through Jesus Christ our Lord. *Amen.*

Eternal God, who hast called us from the busy world to worship thee in quietness, we approach the table of thy Son unworthy even to be near it; for who of us can say he has no need to ask the ancient question,

"Lord, is it I?" Help us to eat the bread in remembrance of the body that was broken for us, and by the drinking of the cup to show forth the Lord's death till he come again in glory. Henceforth let that mind be in us which was in Christ Jesus, and grant also that we may be in him. *Amen.*

## Good Friday

God of all truth, forgive us our deceptions. Offended by the kiss of betrayal, we yet betray thee day by day, and we are without excuse, for we know what we do. Pardon us for the evil we have done and have no power to recall, and save us from the treachery that we shall not avoid except by thy grace. From the cowardice that leads to silence and from the silence that gives consent to injustice, from the pride that breeds impatience and from the impatience that begets faithlessness, from the greed that brings hardness of heart and from the hardness of heart that puts an end to love —good Lord, deliver us, and purge us of our sin through Jesus Christ our Lord. *Amen.*

Bring close the far green hill, our Father, and let not the passing years obscure the agony against the sky. We would not make the cross an ornament, nor remembering the death of thy Son, forget the sins that led him to die. Be ruthless with us if we do not understand the cost of our redemption, and grant that blessed with the free gift of thy love, we may not prove false to him who earned the gift he gave; for we pray in the name of Jesus Christ our Lord. *Amen.*

Almighty and everlasting God, who dost love even the sinner and turns not away from the most unlovely of thy creatures, help us to love as thou hast first loved us. Recall us from the fruitless search for another road to the empty tomb than that of the cross. Save us from the vanity of easy answers to the wrongs we see around us. Teach us the inescapability of sacrifice, the hopelessness of bearing no burdens except our own, the shame of never laying down life for our friends. Give us the courage to die that we may have the right to live. Through Jesus Christ our Lord. *Amen.*

## Easter

Eternal God and mighty Father, who didst raise from his grave thy Son, raise from their graves thy sons. Living, we are so often dead, and unto thee we cry from the sepulchers of fear and hatred, from the tombs of boredom, ignorance, and prejudice. Redeem us by thy saving power, we pray, and rolling back the greedy stone, set free from death the spirits thou didst bring to birth for life in Jesus Christ. *Amen.*

Almighty and eternal God, whose patience is longer than the ages and whose strength more mighty than our grandest dreams of it, we thank thee that thou hast set a limit to thy tolerance. Thou didst suffer thy

Son to be crucified, and day by day thou dost permit the wicked to stand in the judgment and the way of the godly to perish. But thou didst not leave thy Son in the tomb, and age through passing age thou dost tear the sting from death and rob the grave of victory. Alleluia, our Father! All glory be thine that Christ is risen! All praise to thee that dead in him, with him we rise to live forevermore! *Amen.*

Merciful Father, whose might is ever tender and whose power is endlessly patient, forgive us that we have thought thy wisdom halting and thy love incredible. We do not doubt the cross, and we come in hopeless confidence to see the body in the tomb. But meeting thy Son arisen, we do not recognize whom we have met, and seeing the prints of the nails, we disbelieve what we have seen. Forgive us, O Lord, and on this day of resurrection, grant that we may not find thy goodness too good to be true. In Jesus' name. *Amen.*

## Family Sunday

Almighty God, our heavenly Father, in whose family none is unwanted and from whose household no child wanders unsought or alone, grant that we who dwell in families may love as thou hast first loved us. Save us from judging lest we ourselves be judged. Let not the sun go down on our anger; keep us from treating unkindly those who most deserve our kindness; and vouchsafe that taking freely from the common store of fellowship, we may as freely give. Through Jesus Christ our Lord. *Amen.*

Father almighty, who didst see that it was not good for man to be alone and who didst ordain the home to give him peace and joy, grant, we beseech thee, that we may so live in our families that summoned apart, we may still be together, and that being together, we may not be cleft apart. Restrain our impatience. Chasten our disloyalties of thought or word or deed. And in the weary round of daily tasks, renew our spirits day by day, until, serving and being served, loving and being loved, we find on earth the life that earth cannot contain. Through Jesus Christ our Lord. *Amen.*

Hear us, O Lord, as we pray that our homes may be churches. Lead us there to worship thy glory and search for thy truth, there to tell thy gospel and walk in thy will; and teach us so to live with those we love that, loving, we may truly live. Through Jesus Christ our Lord. *Amen.*

## Pentecost

O thou who didst once come to thy church like the rush of a mighty wind and fill its meeting place with news from thy heavenly kingdom, descend upon thy people here assembled. Appear again as tongues of fire, and so touch our hearts with thy Spirit that gathered now in one accord, we may learn to speak thy word in tongues the world will hear; and hearing, understand; and understanding, obey. Through Jesus Christ our Lord. *Amen.*

We have come out to thy church, our Father, and now we pray that thou wilt send thy church out. We seek thee here in prayer, but grant, we beseech thee, that soon we may seek thee in service. It is good for us to dwell in thy courts and to give thee thanks for all thy lovingkindness, but keep us from so rejoicing in thy temple that we have no time for thy tasks; and when we leave our Father's house, let it be upon our Father's business. Through Jesus Christ our Lord. *Amen.*

Eternal God, who didst send thy Son to be on earth the incarnation of thy love, forgive the sins that nailed him to the cross. Let thy church become another flesh for him, a body serving him as hands and feet of old; and grant that speaking, we may speak for him, and doing, do his will. *Amen.*

## Memorial Day

Eternal Father, whose love is longer than the ages and from whose eye no man departs unseen, we call to remembrance the saints who nobly fought of old. Grant, we beseech thee, that they may have rest from their labors. Fill their hearts with thy peace, and from the blest communion where all are one in thee, let their glory shine as stars forevermore. Through Jesus Christ our Lord. *Amen.*

God of might and Father of mercies, who didst ordain that men should dwell in peace upon the earth, forgive thy warring peoples. Save us from the strife that sets brother against brother. Lead hand to reach for hand across the battlelines, and far and wide around the world, let swords be turned to plowshares and spears to pruning hooks. Through Jesus Christ our Lord. *Amen.*

We would remember, Lord. We would remember the faith that led our fathers through their shadowed valleys, kept them firm in darkened hours, and brought them forth at last to stand where thou didst shed thy warming light upon them. Whatsoever things in them were true, whatsoever things were honest, whatsoever things were just, whatsoever things were pure, whatsoever things were lovely, whatsoever things were of good report; if there be any virtue, and if there be any praise, persuade us to think on these things—lest we forget, lest we forget. In Jesus' name. *Amen.*

## Children's Day

Make us childlike, our Father, but not childish. Teach us to trust, and keep us trustworthy. Lead us to be lovable, and guide us into ever larger love. Daily we depend upon thy grace: daily nourish us in graciousness toward those who depend upon us. Through Jesus Christ our Lord. *Amen.*

Eternal Father, in whose sight the child is often wiser than the man and the man more childish than the child, sustain, we pray, our will to be thy children. Defend us from the strength that pulls us into pride, from the pride that lures us into ignorance, and from the ignorance that has lost the wit to recognize its foolishness. Let not the years encrust our minds with haughtiness, or rend our hearts with hatred, or twist our souls with greed. Bestow upon us, being young, the serenities of age; and grant us, being old, the joys of a child. Through Jesus Christ our Lord. *Amen.*

We thank thee, our Father, for the long dependencies of childhood, for the tenderness which thou dost foster through the weakness of the young, and for the revelation of thyself through the comradeship of the home. Hear us as we pray for our children. For their sakes we sanctify ourselves—our bodies, our minds, our hearts, and our souls; and we beseech thee so to guide our steps that none need say of us that the fathers ate sour grapes and the children's teeth were set on edge. In Jesus' name. *Amen.*

## Independence Day

Deliver us, good Lord, from dishonoring the fathers who bought us our freedom. Add not to their sorrows the scorn of their children. Restrain us from casting their pearls before swine or throwing out their holy gifts to dogs. What the centuries have won in lonely pain, let not the hasting moments handle lightly, and save us from such contentment with our rights that we spurn our obligations. Through Jesus Christ our Lord. *Amen.*

Give us independence, our Father, but not of thee. Make us rebels, but not against thy will. Help us to choose our revolutions wisely, and grant that conforming, we conform to thy purpose; that loving, we love thy kingdom; and that serving, we serve no master but thyself. In Jesus' name. *Amen.*

Eternal God, who didst ordain thy people for freedom and who hast no will that any man be bound, let not our independence be an end but a beginning. Save us from the liberty that is better called license; protect us from the arrogance that masquerades as honesty; and vouchsafe that freed from man's bondage, we may be free for thy service. Through Jesus Christ our Lord. *Amen.*

## Labor Day

Almighty God, whose labors have no end and whose rest is ever in the midst of toil, grant to all workers full joy in their work. Let not their bread be earned in drudgery, their satisfaction sought in greed, or their nights made restless by the envy of their brothers. In office or store, in field or factory, in kitchen or schoolroom—vouchsafe that they may find the means of serving thee; and blessing them with awareness of thy need, bless them also with the will to meet it. Through Jesus Christ our Lord. *Amen.*

O thou whose labor is always filled with purpose, save us from the toil that serves unworthy ends. We work to live, but let not our life become the road on which our brothers die. If the daily task adds nothing to the common store of righteousness and joy, if it leads a weaker man to sin, if it fosters strife or cruelty or pain —show us, Lord, the way and give us, Lord, the will to earn our bread by other means. Teach us to love ourselves, but not to suffocation. Make us ambitious, but only for thy kingdom. Through Jesus Christ our Lord. *Amen.*

Eternal Father of us all, who dost long to see thy children love what thou dost love, forgive the sins that bind our hands before the opportunities to share thy daily thrusts toward righteousness. Let the hirer and the hired never stand alone, and grant that they may always face in thee a Third, whose holiness condemns their greed and shames their lust for lordly power. Bend thou all wills to thine, O Lord, and coming to thine altar to praise, may we not depart except to serve. Through Jesus Christ our Lord. *Amen.*

*51*

## Reformation Day

God of grace and God of glory, who hast never left the world without a witness to thy will, we praise thee for the fathers who begot us in the faith. We bless thee for thy Son Jesus Christ, in whom the Word was made flesh; for the earliest disciples, who heard the call to follow and hearing, obeyed; for the stalwart souls who kept thy church alive across the middle years of trial and temptation; and more especially this day for the Protestant Reformers, who preached again the long-forgotten gospel of thy freely given love for man. Let the likeness of the fathers be upon their children, Lord, and grant that being Protestants by birth, we may be as surely Protestants by word and deed. Through Jesus Christ our Lord. *Amen.*

Save us, our Father, from the need for a new Reformation. What thou didst reveal of old in thy Son and set forth anew when Luther walked the earth, and Calvin, let not the years again reduce to relics of an age remembered only by its fossils. If, being believers, we are thy priests, grant that being thy priests, we may truly believe. Teach us to testify for thee in terms the world can understand today, and if, being Protestants, we must deny the false, vouchsafe that, being Protestants, we may as surely reaffirm the true. Through Jesus Christ our Lord. *Amen.*

Merciful Father, have mercy on us. We believe: help thou our unbelief, and by the faith we put in Jesus Christ, save us, we beseech thee—*from* ourselves, *against* ourselves, and *in spite of* ourselves. Grant that being insufficient, we find sufficiency in thee, and that being weak, we hold not back from thy service the weakness whereby thou dost make perfect thy strength. In Jesus' name. *Amen.*

## Thanksgiving

We praise thee, O God. For wind and water we praise thee—for sunlight and starlight, for mountain and field, and for all the wonders of thy hand in earth and sea and sky. For men and women and children we praise thee—for those who share our homes and sustain us with their love, for those who stand beside us in our churchly fellowship and seek with us to walk where Jesus walked of old, for those who live in other lands and by their difference from ourselves proclaim the wideness of thy merciful love. But most of all, we praise thee for thyself—for the will that brought the world to being and broods upon it day by day, for the gift of thy Son and our redemption through his grace, and for thy Holy Spirit and its sanctifying power. Accept our praise, we beseech thee, and guide us till we give thee loyalty no less readily than thanks. Through Jesus Christ our Lord. *Amen.*

Almighty and eternal God, whose goodness is greater even than our sin and whose love exceeds our own unworthiness to ask it, we thank thee for the manifold evidences of thy grace that surround and sustain us. Forgive, we pray, the blindness that looks and looks but never sees, the arrogance that thinks it earns what no man has except by thy free gift, the callousness that feeds upon thy bounty but never wonders what it cost thee to create it. Open our eyes to thy love, and grant that while we praise thee now for what we know of thee, we may learn to praise thee more for all thy glories still unrecognized. Through Jesus Christ our Lord. *Amen.*

Eternal God, whose kindness we have tasted day by day, we praise thee for thy mighty acts and for all thy patience with the children of men. We extol thee for thy power, high and lifted up—holding all creation in the hollow of thy hand. We bless thee for thy wisdom, pure and undefiled—piercing our pretensions with the brightness of thy truth. We thank thee for thy love, steadfast and undiscouraged—caring for us even when we do not care for thee. Forget not, we beseech thee, our need to remember whence cometh our help, and through the abundance of thy favor lead us to the fullness of thy service. In Jesus' name. *Amen.*

# PASTORAL
# PRAYERS

## GENERAL PRAYERS

*For awareness*

Almighty Father, who didst once reveal thyself to men in Jesus Christ and whose Spirit ever moves among us through the days that come and go, we praise thee for the love which has given us the breath and bread of life. Thou art the Lord of the ages, Master of the wheeling stars, Ruler of the distant worlds, and King of all that is or was or evermore shall be. Thou dost work thy will beneath the waters and upon the mountains; thou dost know the lonely skies where man has never been; and before there was time, there was thee, and before there was space, thou didst brood upon the emptiness.

Yet thou dost still concern thyself with man, and trusting in thy love even of the unlovable, we turn to thee in prayer. Hear then the spoken prayers that reach the ears of all who bow before thee in this place, but hear as well the unspoken prayers which rise from hearts which mean them only for thyself—the fearful prayers, the doubting prayers, the confident prayers,

55

the thankful prayers. Let this sanctuary become the threshold of thy presence, where each may see at once the wildness of the world and the wonder of thy peace. In these moments set apart for thy worship, make these walls thy chosen home, a place where thou dost dwell in justice and mercy, a house illumined by thy loving-kindness and a fortress strengthened by thy boundless power.

For all these things and more we pray, our Father, and yet we know that thou hast answered our prayers before we offered them to thee. For thou art in our midst already—more real than this building which houses our worship, more inescapable than the air that we breathe, more intimately related to us than our friends and our neighbors in these pews. And thus we pray less for the assurance that thou *wilt* come than for the awareness that thou *hast* come, and we do not ask for a sunlit sky and a pleasant journey but only for clean sight and loyal faith and strong resolve. Let there be great burdens for our shoulders, and give us the strength to carry them. Let there be hard tasks for our minds, and grant us the wisdom to meet them. Spare us not the peril or the pain of these painful and perilous days, but toiling in the dark, may we live in thy light, and being blessed by thee, may we become a blessing to the world that thou dost love. Through Jesus Christ our Lord. *Amen.*

## For diligence

Almighty and eternal God, who art the Maker of heaven and earth and the Giver of every good and per-

fect gift, from the rush and the roar of our living we
come to thee; from the fever of our striving and the
blindness of our hoping we come to thee; from our joys
and from our sorrows, from our successes and from our
failures, from our assurances and from our doubts we
come to thee. For thou art Way and Truth and Life,
and lost, we see the lights of home before us; false, we
stand corrected; and dead to love and purity, we rise
new creatures in thy sight.

Thou dost bring each day to the dawn, and thou
dost touch the evening with thy peace: save us then
from the need to face the twilight restless in the memory
of hours withheld from thy will. Thou hast made of one
family all the nations of the earth, and thou dost love
each of thy children as if thou hadst no child but him:
help us then to love our brothers as thou hast first
loved us—to love the rich and love the poor, to love
the good and love the bad, to love the wise and love
the foolish. Thou hast compassion on all who are
hungry or cold or in need of any kind, and thou dost
loose thy wrath on all who bring death and despair on
those for whom thou didst plan life and hope: persuade
us then to share thy yoke of tenderness, to give and not
to count the cost, to dare and not to fear the conse-
quence, to love and not to seek reward. By the knowledge of thy Son thou hast set us apart and made us a
chosen people. If thy kindled flame has died within us,
fan it once again to fire, and leave us not alone until
being thy children, we bear upon ourselves the likeness of our Father.

None than thee could better know our waywardness, O God, and in our hearts we bare each secret fault to thy redeeming grace. Repentant, we know thy forgiveness, and going forth from this house which we have committed to thy glory, we shall go with burdens lifted, with strength increased, and with faith restored. Through Jesus Christ our Lord. *Amen.*

## In need of God

We turn toward thee, O Lord, in need of thee. More even than we know, we need thee, and we pray that in this hour thou wilt both make us more aware of our need and open our hearts to thy coming.

In the week that is past, we know that we have often fallen short of the life we intended to live, and silently we confess to thee the stubborn wrongs with which we have affronted thee—the angry words with which we wounded wife or husband, the undeserved impatience with our children, the needless worry inflicted on father or mother, the clever blurring of the truth in passing on the gossip of the neighborhood, the pleasure we found in the misfortunes of our competitors, the nurture of grudges, and the encouragement of malice. Of these sins against thy love we are guilty, our Father, and we are without excuse. We knew better, but still we committed them; and confessing them to thee, we pray that thou wilt deliver us from the will to commit them again.

In the week that lies ahead, we know that we shall bear a heavy burden, Lord, and we ask the strength to carry the load in faithfulness and courage. Give us such confidence in thee that we shall not need to buttress our own security by criticism of our friends. Teach us so to rest upon thy power that we shall not bear the barren freight of fear and worry, so to honor thy creation of ourselves that we shall not be jealous of the work which thou hast done in other men, and so to fasten our lives to thy will that sudden choices do not find us bewildered or unannounced temptations take us by surprise. Should death or bereavement approach us, should accident or other sorrow wait for us along the road, lead us even in the shadowed valley so to walk that we shall one day stand again upon the hills. And in joy or in sorrow, in peace or in pain, in light or in darkness, keep us so close to thyself that knowing thee, we shall love thee, and loving thee, serve thee. Through Jesus Christ our Lord. *Amen.*

## Speak to us

Almighty and eternal God, who dost abide within the ways of men and beyond them, we turn toward thee and pray that in our turning we may see thee not as through a glass and darkly.

Thou knowest the tumult that circles our minds— how we long to understand thee fully but fear the while that, understanding, we shall be compelled to change our cherished habits; how we yearn to put our trust in thee but have not yet the faith that when man loses life in thee, he finds it for himself; how we hunger for some word that cannot be refuted but hear around us only human judgments—fallible, changing, and without the constancy which thou couldst surely give.

Speak to us, Lord, and lead us to listen. Speak to us through all the years that men have known—their victories and their defeats, their exaltation and their abasement, the rise and fall of the nations and peoples, the seers who thought thy thoughts after thee, and the prophets whose words and ways were as thine own. Speak to us through the men and women whom we see about us in the world today—the good and the bad, the wise and the foolish, the rich and the poor, those who are near thee and see from purer hearts what we ourselves have not beheld, and those who are far from thee and teach us once again that hell is any place where man has repulsed thee. Speak to us through mind, or heart, or soul, or whatever that may be which makes it possible for men to have kinship with thee who made them at the first.

Beget in us a thirst for thy presence. Kindle in us the impulse to pray. Tear out our pride; rip away our fear; and persuade us to kneel in our need that we may rise in thy strength.

In this nation grant that we may show our love for thee by working loyally toward justice in every touch of man upon his fellow man. In this church grant that we may willingly become a part of that body wherein again the Word is made flesh and dwells on the earth. Chasten us until we submit to thy will with rejoicing; guide us until we obey thy will without fear; and then so free us from the chains of the days that are gone that forgetting what lies behind and straining forward to what lies ahead, we may press on toward the goal for the prize of the upward call of God in Christ Jesus our Lord. *Amen.*

## Not to slow the kingdom

Almighty and eternal God, whom we seek to find, and sometimes meet in the inward heart but often think we fail to see at all, we thank thee for every sign of thy coming to men. We give thee praise that thou dost speak to us in the coolness of those mornings when all the symphony of heaven and earth is pouring forth the word that this is thy world, in the fellowship of kindred minds when the touch of life on life renews our knowledge that in the beginning thou didst make us as we are, in the record of the years gone by when history confirms our faith that only truth can triumph or justice long endure.

Thou knowest that we do not always seek thee with the faithfulness thou dost deserve. Thou knowest, too, how much our sin has dimmed the windows of our souls until no sudden need of thee can bring the sight of thee for which we long. Yet we turn to thee in trust because thou wast at Gethsemane when the sweat of thy Son was like great drops of blood falling down upon the ground; and thou wast at Calvary when the cross was raised on the windy hill; and knowing our weakness, thou knowest no less the weight of the load and the length of the climb.

Purge us, then, of the fear that shortens our vision. Strip us of the pride that saps our strength. Cleave us from the greed that wastes our life in the effort to save it. Grant that we may be sensitive to thy people everywhere, but spare us the folly of not seeing what lies close at hand. Make us generous in helping those across the seas, but lead us also to help the man next door. Guard us against hating our enemies, but protect us, too, from neglecting our friends. Give us grace to toil for peace among the nations, but allow us no contentment until we end the wars in our homes.

We pray for ourselves, our Father, but as we grow in strength and sight, we pray that we may also grow in eagerness to serve thy will for other men. Accept us as thy servants, Lord, that we may be thy sons and daughters, too. Bend us in thy bondage that we may at last be free. And vouchsafe that in the end we may not slow thy kingdom's coming to the earth. Through Jesus Christ our Lord. *Amen.*

## For those in special need

O thou Spirit high and holy, Creator of the universe, and Maker of man, we come before thee not as individuals and not as an audience but as a congregation of those who love thee and who seek to serve thee. Not one in outward being, neither are we one in thought or word or deed, and gathered in thy presence, we are as many as the heads we bow in thy praise. Yet we have pledged ourselves to thee in the fellowship of this church and taken covenant among ourselves to walk in peace and helpfulness together, and so this day we lift to thee the prayers of all of us for the sake of each of us, and more especially for those who need thee most of all.

If there is one among us facing surgery of which he stands in dread, one crushed by tasks for which he thinks himself incompetent, one walking daily in the shadow of a fate unwanted or unknown—we pray for him. Grant him to know that when we fear, we bear the burden of a multitude of ills that never come to pass. Vouchsafe that he may find the rock of spirit undergirding all the frailties of flesh. And should some loss of hope again assail him, lead him then to lean himself upon thy mighty arm and know that naught has yet been met by man which thou couldst not bring man to meet in victory.

If there is one among us who has lost his grip on life's meaning, who knows not who he really is or where his life is headed or what he ought to do and why—we pray for him. Speak thou to him this day and help him to understand that it was thee who brought him forth from his mother's womb and destined him for life on earth. Stir him to seek the larger meanings of the work by which he earns his daily bread, to serve thy kingdom first, and to keep in lesser place the things which earth can give and take away. Let him find his calling in thy will, and grant him strength to answer it in all he thinks and says and does.

If there is one among us bitter in the death of one

he loved, or hurt by faithlessness of friends, or soured by the thought that life has not bestowed on him the living he deserves—we pray for him. Reveal to him that thou canst have a purpose for his life beyond the pleasures of his body and the satisfaction of his known desires. Lead him into awareness of the host of times when he has stood in need of pardon on his own. And in the losses he sustains grant him to judge aright the welfare of the ones who die and his selfishness in wanting them to remain longer beside him.

For these and all men else who live in special need of thee this day we raise our prayers to thee, our Father, and we ask that thou wilt so bind the hearts of all of us in Christian love that we may be a channel of thy grace to each of us. Through Jesus Christ our Lord. *Amen.*


## For the world

We pray for the world, our Father. We pray for that world which thou didst find so dear that it was worth the giving of thy Son. We pray for all of the world, the lands we know but also those other lands that stand within our minds as nothing more than names. Each of them is thine, and all the people in them are thy children; and for all of them we pray that life may be their lot and not death, peace and not war, righteousness and not the ways of wickedness and wrong.

We pray for our brothers in the faith who bear the heaviest burdens of discipleship in foreign fields or in the harder pastures of their native land. Through every peril of their road be thou their strength and hope, and though the world should be removed from them, grant them still to know their lodging in thy love and in that lodging not to be afraid.

We pray for our enemies—the humble folk among them who want war no more than we ourselves nor have as much as we the power to thrust the chance of war away, but the arrogant among them, too, the ones who need thy guidance if ever men have needed it and in whom now, if ever, men need to find thy hardy goodness surging. We pray for the beaten and the broken, the hungry and the harried, the sad and the sorrowing, the lost and the lonely. Be thou in them as man can never be, to comfort them, uphold them, and redeem them.

Yet save us from believing that because we ask that thou shouldst succor them, thou dost not use us as the instruments of what we ask of thee. Vouchsafe that we may be thine earthly hands and feet and that thy holy ministry may find its issue in some deed we do of mercy, some act of justice, some healing ordinance of love.

For most of all, O Lord, we pray for ourselves, and we ask that thou wilt teach us how much depends on those who say they want to be thy servants. Give us the bravery to face without deception what we truly are and ought to be. Reveal to us anew what things are good and what things bad, what things great and what things small, what things deserve our hearts' devotion and what other things, though prized by the mighty, are none the less no more than impertinent trinkets among the honest jewels of thy grace. And then grant us the will to do the things we know we ought to do. Let thy will become of greater moment to us than the prejudices of our fellows, and though the times be fair or foul, lead on, thou King eternal, until we stand at last on ground unmoved, immovable. For we pledge thee faith and faithfulness, and where thou art, we, too, would be. Through Jesus Christ our Lord. *Amen.*

## Confession and petition

O thou Father almighty, Maker of heaven and earth and Giver of all that we have and all that we are, hear our prayers, we beseech thee, and so respond to them both now and through the days to come that we may know that thou hast heard and that thou dost will for us what will be best for us.

We confess to thee that in the week that lies behind us, our feet have often wandered from the ways in which we wish they might have gone. We have been noisy when we ought to have been still. We have been anxious when we ought to have been calm. We have been angry with our children when we ought to have been patient. We have been unkind, untrue, unloving; and our memories are burdened with regrets and the knowledge of failure. We cannot make deeds done as never having happened, but thou canst break their hold upon us and lift us up to walk again in faith where thou wouldst have us go. And so we speak to thee our hidden faults, and ask of thee thy pardon, and take from thee the healing of thy love.

Abide with us in coming days, our Father, and grant us in this church to be a company of those who love thee, and loving thee, serve thee, and serving thee, learn to love thee even more. Confront us with a common purpose, and in the need to make thy will effective in the world, teach us to work together. Deny us satisfaction with a life whose limits are no larger than ourselves. Guard us from the envy of our neighbors that is rooted in our own lack of security, and lead us day by day in better understanding of who we really are, why we are here, and where we are going.

Protect us from the false humility which shrinks from action lest its weakness be revealed, and fortify our courage until we gladly offer talent as we have it and neither minimize nor overestimate the contribution which we make. Lead us to see aright the imperfections in ourselves, and seeing them, to find in other people's faults the reason neither for astonishment nor for revulsion. Defend us alike from thinking that we can save the world by our own strength and from succumbing to despair because we cannot.

We pray for ourselves, O Lord, but only that we may become better instruments of thy purpose. Command us, we pray; empower us; enlighten us; lead us. Through Jesus Christ our Lord. *Amen.*

## *For our comrades and ourselves*

O thou eternal Spirit, thou whom eye hath not seen nor ear heard, we turn our thoughts toward thee, and we pray that in the hidden deeps of heart and soul thou wilt manifest thyself to us. Thou art a God of mystery, and thou wilt ever be high and lifted up above the common ways we know. Yet thou hast said through Christ that where two or three are gathered together in thy name, thou wilt be in the midst of them, and thou hast said through him that they who seek shall surely find. Here, then, in this thy house, be known of us, and grant that we shall never again believe that we are cleft from thee.

We pray for our comrades seated in the pews near by: for the aged, whose days upon the earth seem often numbered, whose bodies are enfeebled and whose powers are withdrawn; for the young, whose ways are unsettled and whose goals are unsure, whose minds are troubled and whose hearts are beset; for those not young and not yet old, who currently bear the world's sorest burdens of duty and toil, who know how many dreams of their youth will never have life and who see the ruts of the past traversing the fields of the future. We pray for the restless of spirit and the anxious of soul; for those who face some dreaded test of faith or strength and know not whether they will rise or fall; for those whose loved ones are in danger, or illness, or hardship of any kind; and for any other man, or woman, or child on whom a crushing load has now been laid. Bestow on these and all other members of this congregation that wisdom which thou alone canst give and that peace which the world can neither grant nor take away.

But we pray, too, for ourselves. We know the need for brotherhood and peace, and we hear the call that thou dost give through Christ to all who make his name their own. One by one reveal to us, we beseech thee, the deeds which we can do to serve both him and thee. Save us from thinking so much about the mighty works beyond our power that we have no time for work within our reach. Keep us from demanding perfection so soon that we will not take the lesser tasks by which alone it comes to pass. Keep thou our eyes on distant lands and lofty heights, but lead us, too, to see our neighbor in his need and scale the hills that lie near by, until being faithful over little things, we are strong enough at last to be faithful over greater things. Through Jesus Christ our Lord. *Amen.*

## For a heart of compassion

Almighty and eternal God, who art the Author of life and the Father of men, the earth is thine and the fullness thereof, the world and they that dwell therein. Thou dost ordain the stars in their courses and the seasons that wheel in their ceaseless round. Thou hast blessed us with thy favor so that none need be in want or be lonely, and thou hast granted us such knowledge of thyself that we need not fear though the earth be removed and the mountains carried into the midst of the sea.

Therefore it is upon thee that we call in the days when the waters of the world are troubled and the floods of passion loose themselves among the sons of men, and we pray for wise minds, and valiant hearts, and souls made strong by the touch of thy Spirit. We would be faithful, our Father, and true and kind; but thou hast brought us into being in a wilderness of cruelty and pain, and we know not what to do. We would be helpful, our Father, and err not, neither wander from thy way; but we have fallen into days of darkness and despair, and our vision ends before the road to hope begins. In the wilderness prepare, we beseech thee, a way, and on the dark send down thy light, so that marching sometimes in blindness, we may yet march in faith, and striving always in weakness, we may yet add our little strength to thy prevailing might.

O thou who art the source of all that is or was or evermore shall be, give us a heart of compassion for our fellows. Lead us to put reins on the wild horses of our pride and bridles on the mad steeds of our hatred lest, turning, they trample us down in their fury and crush thy will that we become thy comrades in the healing of the nations. Teach us to covet for ourselves only that which will hasten the coming of thy kingdom and to seek for our foes nothing which will slow our common restoration to the circle of thy love. Open our hearts and our hands that from the storehouses of our abundance we may give of thy bounty to all who are hungry or cold or homeless. And through the confusion and terror of these days give us wisdom so to live together on the earth that war shall lift its ugly head no more, but peace reign, and justice triumph, and brotherhood abide. In Jesus' name. *Amen.*


## God almighty

God almighty, God eternal, God of mercy, God of love, God abiding ever in the universe of thy creation and ever watching over all the men and women thou hast given breath of being: vainly have we sought thee in the places where thou goest not, and coming here to this thy chosen house, we strive again to find the knowledge we have lost or never reached. Thou art all the life we have—all the strength and all the hope, all the light and all the peace—and as we turn to thee, we know that we are turning toward a fountain springing forth from rocks eternal and that drinking from the waters thou dost freely give, our hearts are made clean within us and our souls renewed and opened to thy bidding.

Grant then that here among those whom we know and love, here among those whom we know and do not love, and here among those whom we do not know or even care to know, the prayers of each may be a blessing to all and the earnestness of all, the healing of each. Open our hearts, our Father. Open our hearts. Open our hearts. Examine them thyself and see them as they truly are, and then, as if thou didst extend thy hand to us and lead us to the brink of cliffs of which we were afraid, persuade us that we face ourselves as thou hast seen us to be. Help us to understand how frail we are, how fearful, how firmly fettered with the chains of pride and greed, of lust and hatred. Open our hearts, our Father. Open our hearts. Open our hearts. Let the healing winds flow over them until their fevered restlessness has died away, and then with gladness let us walk the road of life again—eager but not anxious, troubled but not dismayed, seeing often dimly but never wholly blind, and always sure that thou canst use our weakness to magnify thy power. Let our peace be that of ships borne up on mighty waters, and let our struggles be like those of great planes rising skyward on the air which, never seen, yet gives support to wings that rest themselves upon it. For thus shall all our life be praise of thee, and what we think or say or do be offerings upon thine altars; and the whole, wide world shall own thee Lord, and men be brothers once again as once thou madest them of old. Through Jesus Christ our Lord. *Amen.*

## Thou knowest this parish

Thou knowest this parish, our Father. Thou knowest this congregation gathered here to worship thee. Thou knowest the heart of each who bows his head in thy presence. And what we have been, and what we are, and what we long to be, thou understandest even better than we do ourselves.

We come to thee proud but not having reason to be proud. We come to thee afraid but not knowing where to turn in search of confidence. We come to thee aching with the weariness of trying to live nobly but conscious always that we have not lived as nobly as we should. There is bitterness among us; there is hatred; there are loneliness and guilt, pain and the dread of pain, lust and greed and despair. We need thee, Lord. Each man and woman among us, each boy and girl in our midst—we need thee, and for each of us we pray as if we prayed for him alone, and each of us for all. Gird thou with strength the ones who face this week some hardship unforeseen. Calm thou with peace the ones who have not learned that thou art Lord of all. Fire thou with holy purpose those who live as if their only ends were self-content, their only purpose peace.

We shall not be burned at stakes, our Father, nor thrown to beasts of prey, nor even cast in prison for the faith we say we have in thee. All the more freely therefore teach us to bear our proper witness in the hours that come and go. On the Sabbath day let unexpected visitors be shown our love of thee because we go to church despite their coming—and take them with us. When conflicts come between the world and thee, grant us not to choose the world. Help us to lead our children in thy ways by going first ourselves where we would have them go, and save us from believing that our little ones are likely to be found in heaven if their parents live in hell. Give us the courage to speak about the things in which we think that we believe. Let

73

"Good luck!" be less upon our lips than "God bless you!" And for the daily sustenance of body and mind, for muscle and nerve, for heart and brain and soul, spur us to bless the One from whom they came, that day by day we may know thee more perfectly, love thee more completely, and serve thee more faithfully. Through Jesus Christ our Lord. *Amen.*

## So high and lifted up

It is so hard for us to think of thee, our Father, so hard for us to picture thee, so hard for us to feel thy presence as we do the presence of a friend whom we can see and touch and hear. Thou art so high, so lifted up, so pure and wonderful in all thy ways that thou seemest almost past our understanding altogether.

Yet we know that thou art closer to us than breathing and nearer than hands and feet, and even when we doubt thee, we know that it is thee who givest us the strength to doubt. So once again, in fellowship with those who share our vows and hopes with us, we bow before thee, we become quiet before thee, and pulling back as best we can the thoughts that wander far away from thee, we fix our minds on thee and pray that thou wilt heal our hearts and make them whole. For we are so worried, Lord, so anxious, so fretful. We are hurried, yet we have eternity. We are afraid, yet we have thee. We wish we knew thy will for us, yet in Christ thou givest us the very knowledge which we seek and say we do not have.

74

Come now to this portion of thy people, we pray. Descend upon this congregation. Be known of this church. And in the heart of each of us be not an idea only, a theory, a thought, a hope, or a dream. Be thou a being met and known. Persuade us into praying, and out of our prayers bring forth that knowledge which the world can neither give nor take away, that confidence which has no fear of life or death, that peace which passes understanding and is not moved by any awfulness which man conceives or undertakes.

What we can do to make the world more nearly as thou didst intend it, reveal to us, our Father; and what we comprehend of thy will for us, grant us to obey. Lead us till our daily work becomes an instrument for high and holy things. Transform our homes that they may be the seedbeds of thy purpose. Chasten our souls until they know the joy of sacrifice. And bring us in the end to love thee with all our hearts and to serve thee with all our strength. Through Jesus Christ our Lord. *Amen.*

## That light may shine

O thou Father of might and of mercy, in whom our spirits have their home both now and evermore, we lift up our hearts to thee in this hour and seek in thee the peace that man can neither give nor take away, the life that counts its losses gain if they be suffered for the sake of Jesus Christ. We see thee in the far-flung stars of night and in the goodly sun by day. We see thee where the mountains lift their heads to touch the skies and in the valleys where the rich earth brings forth the bounty of thy love. We see thee in the life of man with man, in the common toil of kindred souls, in the holy comradeship of hearth and home, in the love that leaps the battlelines of human strife and binds us even to the enemies whose wills we must oppose. We see thee in the one whom thou didst send to show thy life to men, the carpenter who spoke in Galilee the word the whole world heard, Jesus Christ, thy Son, our Lord. If we ascend up into heaven, thou art there; and though we make our bed in hell, behold, even there we find thy footsteps close beside us.

Grant then, God, that what we see in everything around us we may in truth believe and love. Spare us the anguish of searching the world for what lies at our feet. Thou art far away, ruler of the stars in their courses and master of worlds beyond our sight or dream; but thou art near us, too, inside the reach of our hands, firm in the depths of our hearts. Cause us then to know that thou art ever nigh, that we face no hardship and bear no pain alone, and that in every circumstance of our living and our dying thou art here to bless and save. We stand by the still waters of thy peace, and we long that our thirst be quenched: teach us to bend the knee to drink what thou hast bent thyself to bestow.

And then, having peace ourselves, our Father, vouchsafe that we may be free for the tasks to which thou dost summon thy people day by day. Tear down the hesitations by which we enfeeble our love. Remove the thought of gain from the service we offer thy kingdom. Call us where thou wilt. Give us victory if victory will serve thee best, or bring us to the end of our hope if by despair thou canst more surely accomplish thy will. Establish us in some place where the needs of men cry out for strength beyond themselves, and there let thy light so shine through us that seeing thee, men may also love thee, and loving thee, forsake their foolish ways and come at last to their home in thy care. Through Jesus Christ our Lord. *Amen.*

## *For faithfulness in serving*

Father almighty, thou Spirit high and holy who dwellest where the farthest stars obey their given way, but livest, too, where man meets man among us here, we leave our daily tasks behind and turn alone to thee. Thou knowest how we need thee, how we wait for thee as watchmen wait for the morning, how we faint and fall without thee. Yet thou knowest also how we fear thee, how we dread thy light and lordship, how we keep thee out lest, coming in, thou shouldst humble us and make as dust our pomp and pride.

O seize us for thy purpose, Lord; command us for thy will; and making us thy prisoners, set us truly free. Give us sympathy with other men, and excusing our own failures because of headaches, bad stomachs, or troubles at home, grant us as great a patience with those who offend us. Lead us to think the best of our fellows and not the worst, and save us from the arrogance which prevents us from loving anyone whose opinions do not coincide with our own beliefs. Keep us from the folly of saving our faces by losing our souls, and if we have wronged another man, give us here and now the will to admit the wrong and ask for pardon. Allow us no peace if we have built our self-esteem on the abuse of a brother, and protect us from bearing false witness against our neighbors by telling lies as if they were the truth or by so telling the truth that it serves as a lie. And then so free us from the fear of trusting ourselves to thy hands that in the awareness of thy love we find all the security we need and in thy service all the peace.

Thou hast given us life in twisted times, our Father, and being in need, we have prayed for ourselves; but we ask for thy blessings only that, receiving, we may give. Grant us to be strong that our might may be a bulwark to those who are weak. Grant us to be wise that our wisdom may shed a needed light upon a darkened way. Grant us to be brave that our courage may bring hope in a day of despair. For we now commit to thee both our life and our death, and pledging thee faith, we pledge thee, too, our faithfulness. Through Jesus Christ our Lord. *Amen.*

## We would see Jesus

Almighty and eternal God, who didst so love the world that thou gavest thy Son for our life and salvation, we turn to thee in the splendor of the morning and

78

lift up our hearts to thy glory. A thousand years in thy sight are but as yesterday when it is past and as a watch in the night, and from everlasting to everlasting thou remainest unchanged and unchanging. Yet no sparrow's fall escapes thy knowledge, and thou lovest each of thy children as if he alone were thy child. We make bold therefore to draw nigh unto thee and to pray that, drawing nigh unto us in thy turn, thou wilt lead us into the saving grace of Jesus Christ our Lord.

Our hearts are troubled, Lord, and our minds are rent by embattled loyalties, torn by unruly passions, shamed by unwanted memories, imperiled by alluring temptations. We are not one but many, and the noble does war with the base, and we know not where our sure hope lies. We have no doubt that we need thee, but we need thee even more than we know; and because the world is so much with us, we ask for clearer sight of him whom thou didst send to overcome the world.

We would see Jesus, the man whom thou didst lead to earth to live in love among the hateful, to be at peace in the midst of the wrangling, and to walk in faith through the hosts of the fearful. We would be Bethlehem, our Father. We would be Nazareth, Capernaum, and Calvary; and as thy Son is born anew and as he dwells again where once he dwelt, we would stand so close to him that we need never doubt his life nor ever fear our death.

But we would also see Christ, the man who was more than a man, the Word made flesh and moving daily where men daily walked yet ever rising swiftly past their feeble sight. The walls of ignorance imprison our knowledge, but we pray that thou wilt give gates to our vision. The fogs of sin destroy our faith, but we ask that thou wilt split the skies and drive the mists away. Teach us so to see thy Son that we may see thee, so to live in him that neither life nor death can cleave us from thy love, and so to die for his sake that we may live forevermore. *Amen.*

## If accident or illness

O thou God of the ages and Father of men, thou who art as near us as breath and yet so courteous in thine approach to us that we could live through all our days and neither recognize thee nor admit thee, thou beyond whom nothing is and of whose will there is no end in time or space, thou who art more patient than the stars and greater in thy love than any man on earth or all the men on earth—we thank thee that thou hast not long since thrust us from this world of thy creation. Thou hast given us so much beauty and splendor, so many causes for rejoicing and gratitude, so great abundance of the riches both of body and of mind; but we have wasted thy substance in fatuous living, poured down the drains of neglect what thou didst bring to being in travail and hope, turned proud backs on all that seemed to thee the ends and aims of human striving rightly undertaken.

Chasten us, Lord, that we may see clearly. Humble

us that we may stand firmly. Arouse us that we may wake from self-concern and in surrender to thy serfdom win the liberty of those who put their trust in thee.

The days are dark before us, and because we cannot know what lies in wait for us, we pray that thou wilt gird us lest we meet them unprepared. If accident or illness be our lot in coming weeks, grant us to face them unafraid and through their idleness and pain find new fellowship with thee, new understanding of the multitudes whose daily battlefields are beds of agony or helplessness. If some fresh blessing hovers near our doors, vouchsafe that we may welcome it with humble thankfulness and hold in merciful compassion the hosts of other men who, no less deserving than ourselves, are yet less obviously favored. If death be near, help us to meet it with the confidence of those who know that death is not the end, and should a loved one die, lead us to bid farewell to him as to a man whose journey is to pleasant places, to have no doubt that he is still thy child, and to leave him in thy care without dismay. If some new need of us is soon to be revealed to us, empower us to recognize it as in fact from thee; prod us until we meet it; and in the meeting of it grant that we may learn to know thee more surely, to love thee more unselfishly, and to trust thee more completely.

Thou art our Father, and we are the creatures of thy will. To thee we dedicate the little strength we have, and we pray that thy kingdom may have use for our weakness. Through Jesus Christ our Lord. *Amen.*

*In the quiet of the evening*

Everlasting and most merciful God, we come to thee in the quiet of the evening, and we pray that thou wilt be to us as the shadow of a great rock in a weary land. All the day long thy love has blessed us on our way, and from the time of our birth until now thou hast ever been our fortress and our might. Through the coming watches of the dark thou wilt guard us still, and no dread hour has ever laid its shroud upon us without the word from thee that thou art victor over all.

Sometimes we know thee and know that we know; sometimes we search afar for thee when thou art as the air we breathe, the ground on which we stand; sometimes we find and sometimes fail to find. Yet always through our struggle and our striving we know that thou dost seek to fend from us the evil that besets us, to cut from us the chains that keep us bound, to drive from us the gloom that clouds our day.

Be with us, then, while the night descends around us. Illumine our hearts with thy glory, and grant that nevermore the dark may have its way with them. Steady our anxious minds; cool our fevered spirits; strengthen our tired hands; and in each touch we have upon our fellows vouchsafe that we may so be ruled by thee that peace may be among us, and justice, and joy.

For we ask thy blessing on others than ourselves this night—those who lie on beds of loneliness or pain in hospital or home or rented room; those who face this week some trial greater than their seeming power to meet and put behind them; the uprooted hosts in lands beyond the seas, the hungry and hurt, the cold and desolate; the young who scan the world and wonder where to find a place in it; and the old who scan the world and wonder if their living has been vain. Grant, Lord, that each who has a need of thee this night may see the answer to his need in thee and, seeing it, may open wide a door through which thou canst come in to him, and sup with him, and he with thee. Through Jesus Christ our Lord. *Amen.*

## Cleanse our hearts

O thou who hast in Christ made thyself known to the world and who in daily life dost still reveal thyself to those who truly seek thy face, we gather here this day in the prayer that this place set apart may be a place set apart to thy will. We live so often in ignorance of what we ought to do and what we ought to say. We fasten our hearts so frequently on that which, having, we should be the poorer for the having; and so many times we think that we are serving thee when in deepest truth we only add another thorn to thy crown, thrust another spear in thy side. Yet the evil we have done we would not always do, and coming here that we may be more surely children of thy grace, we pray that thou wilt separate us from our sin lest, sinning, we be separate from thee.

Cleanse our hearts of evil motive. Fashion us as thou didst intend us—people gladly owning thee as Father, freely saying that we have no strength but thine, and unreservedly committing what we have to ends which merit thine approval. Lead us to see ourselves as thou dost see us—men and women who have sinned alike in ignorance and malice, creatures who have fallen from the heights on which thou didst once implant them, but children still of thine and loved and holy in thy sight. Keep us low enough in thought of self to understand how much we owe to thee, how helpless all our striving is unless it has the surging of thy might beneath it. Yet save us, too, from the loss of self-respect which gives birth to arrogance, unfriendliness, and fear.

O shake the stiffness from our souls, our Father. Cause us to be again as little children, looking at the world with eyes unprejudiced and still unclouded by the films of insecurity, or pride, or hatred of our fellow man. Help us to reinterpret what we see but do not recognize, to reassign the authorship of that to which we sometimes say there is no author, and in the end to live as those who know that thou art both our origin and destiny and that, shouldst thou remove thyself from us, we should be ourselves removed. Through Jesus Christ our Lord. *Amen.*

## Outward from ourselves

Outward from ourselves we turn our hearts this day, our Father, to those who stand in need of thee no less than we and in this moment even more.

We pray for the sick of the parish, those who lie at home as we meet here, and hunger for their health but do not find it; those who are confined to nursing homes and hospitals; those who soon must undergo an operation, face some treatment deeply dreaded, be told of illness which no skill of man can conquer. Thou knowest their loneliness, and we know—their fears, their feebleness of body, their fretfulness of mind. Be thou in them, we pray, and make them know that thou art in them. Fill their hearts with confidence, their souls with trust in thee, their flesh and bones with healing power; and insofar as mind can be of use to mind, vouchsafe that gathered here today, we may release new strength for them and through thee lift them upward out of weakness into health.

We pray for the troubled of the parish, those who have lately been cleft from some loved one deeply cherished; those who have been faced today with arguments and quarrels in their homes; those whose friends have been disloyal, or whose faith has proved unsound, or whose dreams have been destroyed; those who see but dimly what thou dost ask of them and seem each day to slip backward as fast and as far as once they climbed forward. Take the sympathy we offer up to thee in this hour, the love and care and compassion, and let them be a blessing to these people, Lord. Grant to all the troubled of the parish the comfort of a faith with broad horizons. Spare them the needless load of doubting thee, and through the twilight of their worry and their pain send down thy light of trust and hope. And in the words we speak to them and the deeds we do for them, lead them to find such proof of thy care that death has no terror and life no dismay.

We pray for the strong of the parish, those whose loads are great and whose backs are great enough to carry them; those whose bodies are unweakened by illness and whose minds are unassailed by doubt; those whose hands hold reins of power, wielding influence beyond the dreams of the hosts who surround them. Save them, we pray, from accepting these gifts from thee as if they gave them to themselves. Keep them from falling asleep in their own contentment. Protect them from looking squarely at injustice and misery but never really seeing either and never understanding that he who sees and what he sees could be related.

The rich and the poor among us, the strong and the weak, the learned and the unlettered, the young and the old—let each of us and each of them so bend ourselves to thy commands that we shall never stand so straight as when we bow before thy throne; and held in faith by thee and bound in love within thy holy church, we pray that thou wilt grant us both the wisdom and the will to live in fruitfulness the life thou

givest us to live on earth. Through Jesus Christ our
Lord. *Amen.*

## *Receive us, we pray*

O thou who hadst a form when the world was
still formless and void and when darkness was still on
the face of the deep, thou who didst bring forth order
out of chaos, and out of the dust of the ground all
the children of men, thou who canst perform any deed
which can be performed and who so lovest all of us
that thou wilt do for each of us whatever is right and
true and good—as much as in us lies, we pull our
hearts from the ways of the world and fix them in thy
love and law. If never in the week that is gone and if
never in the week that is yet to be lived, now at least,
O Lord, let us enter into conscious fellowship with
thee.

Give us this day our daily bread, but above all of
the needs of our bodies, be patient with those of our
souls. Make us to lie down in green pastures, and lead
us beside the still waters, but before thou bringest us
to peace, lure us into faithfulness. We do not see thee,
our Father. We do not hear thee as we hear the voices
of our fellows in the world. Grant none the less that we
may know thee, and through the day and through the
night so touch our souls that thou dost become a
presence trusted, loved, obeyed.

Save us from so drugging ourselves with sight and

sound that we blur the very vision we have tried to sharpen. In the thirst to pledge allegiance, keep us from setting up false kings on our thrones. In the quest for happiness, guide us out of dead-end streets, and restrain us when we want to sell our souls for that which, belonging at last to ourselves, has robbed us of the selves to which it belongs. Thou art ever in our midst and always by our side: grant then that we may recognize thy presence, receive thy comradeship with gladness, and find in thy love such wealth of strength and peace that whatever else the world may take away, we stand unharmed because we still have all.

Such is the prayer we lift to thee this day, Lord, and we know that thou didst understand our need before we told thee of it. Yet greater than all our other needs is the need we have of thee. Receive us, we pray. Forgive us. Renew us. Through Jesus Christ our Lord. *Amen.*

## By whose mercy we live

Almighty and eternal God, by whose mercy we live and in whose will is our peace, we gather in this holy place, and in company with those whose need is like our own, we strive to thrust the things of earth aside and let these moments be as if we dwelt with thee alone. The world is so much with us, and its sights and sounds so crowd our days that thou must often find our busy inns too full for thee. All the more earnestly, therefore, we dedicate this hour to casting the merchant in us out of us, the anxious householder, the busy husband and father, the worried housewife, the hurried citizen and neighbor; and standing in thy sight only as the humble creatures of thy love, we wait in patience for thy coming to our hearts.

Lift up our eyes to far horizons, Lord, and keep us from the folly of so beholding only what lies at our feet that we never see the sun of hope rising above the mountains before us, nor ever understand that thou hast given us eternity to learn and grow, to comprehend and appreciate, to achieve and attain. Save us alike from attempting the impossible and from calling impossible anything which we have found to be trying. Deny us the false comfort of judging ourselves by our motives and our neighbors by their deeds; and when we think about others, let it be in the consciousness that those who are not against thee are for thee, and when we consider ourselves, grant us the awareness that he who is not with thee is against thee. Let not our condemnation be that we have held a jewel in our hands and thought it only rubble, and blessing us with daily love and sustenance, bless us, too, with knowledge of the gifts thou dost bestow on us, until in humble gratitude we find life's deepest meanings in our present life and feel no more the need to search for what already we possess.

If there is hatred within us, our Father, let there be love; if there is worry, let there be peace; if there is danger, let there be patience. And if we still are blind to the obligations of our stature and possessions in a world still prostrate and distraught, open our eyes until, seeing, we comprehend, and, comprehending, we provide the hands by which alone thou canst perform thy holy will upon the earth. Through Jesus Christ our Lord. *Amen.*

## We commit ourselves

O thou eternal Father of us all, who didst create us in the beginning and dost renew us day by day, we thank thee for the incredible gift of human life and for thy steady grace in keeping us alive. We say to thee in penitence that we have not always done with faithfulness the work which thou hast given us to do, nor ever had the will to lift thy purpose higher than our own. We have left undone what we ought to have done, and even when we have sought to do thy will, we have chosen the right goals for the wrong reasons or tried to build a holy house with bent and rusted tools.

O clarify our thinking, Lord. Cause us to have a just and proper self-regard, and not to treat as rubbish all that thou didst lay down life to bring to being; but save us from loving ourselves to very death. Give us due concern for what happens within our homes and families, but let us see no less the meaning of our lives for other men. Grant us the decency of gratitude for what our fathers taught us of Christ and his kingdom, but keep us from the judgment that we were parasites upon the past, that we took but did not give, and that life came down to us but never went beyond us.

Thou hast a place for each of us—the handsome and the plain, the strong and the weak, the rich and the poor, the hopeful and the frightened. Help us to find that place, and in our fellowship with our brothers in thy household, teach us how little in thy sight is all that cleaves the best of us from the worst of us and the feeblest from the stoutest. If we are strong, lead us to use our strength as those who know it comes from thee; and if we are weak, prevent us from forgetting that thou hast often worked thy will through frailty and sent thy thunder to the world in voices still and small.

As surely as we can, we give ourselves into thy keeping, our Father. We commit ourselves to thy care, and, trusting thy power, thy wisdom, and thy love, we promise thee again to be the heralds of thy kingdom. Through Jesus Christ our Lord. *Amen.*


## As each has need of thee

Almighty and eternal God, who regardest more the silent thoughts of the heart than the words given voice by the lips and who knowest the lives of all as if they were books left open to thy sight, we turn to thee. One body in thy love, we are still the separate children of thy grace, and, praying to thee now, each prays as each has need of thee.

*91*

We call to remembrance thy goodness to us in the days that are past. The holy gift of life itself with its joys and its sorrows, its victories and its defeats, its struggle and its quietness; the comradeship of those who share the sheltered hours of hearth and home, who know the depths to which our souls descend but never lose their faith that we shall scale the heights again; the friendly intercourse of kindred minds in work and play; the chosen yokes we bear with thee on roads of justice, love, and sacrifice; the needed deeds that ask to be done, the kindly words that beg to be spoken, the far horizons that wait to be crossed—for these provisions of thy bounty and for all else that comes in mercy from thy hand we give thee thanks and praise, our Father.

In the silence of this hallowed place we sit, and from these well-loved walls we reach in thought and prayer to all whose need of thee we know—to the sick and the aged of this church and community who hunger for the former, fairer days of health and strength; to those who stand at the noon of their days, whose backs are weary with the burdens they bear, whose hearts are heavy with some special bewilderment or particular grief; to those whose day is at its dawn, children and young people who scan the skies for signs of hope but fear that night will fall before their morning fully comes; to honest statemen trying gallantly to steer their ships toward truth and right while finding all around them only angry clouds and sneering winds and hungry seas; to friendly folk in warring lands who seek a bridge but see a wall, who long to help but go on hurting, who want to walk together but continue to walk alone.

Long since, O Lord, we pledged ourselves to love thee with all our heart and mind and soul and strength. Grant us wisdom, we pray. Give us courage; make us faithful; and then vouchsafe that, loving thee, we may love our neighbor, too. Through Jesus Christ our Lord. *Amen.*


## *Upon whose rock*

O thou upon whose rock thy church is founded, again we draw apart as those who love thee; we turn our minds to seek thy will; and we pray that thou wilt so reveal thyself to us in this hour that we may henceforth see a little more clearly, think a little more wisely, and serve a little more faithfully. We thank thee for the ties that bind our hearts in Christian love and for the host of attitudes and purposes which we unite to speed thy kingdom's coming in this holy fellowship. We thank thee that we are not duplicates of each other and that our comradeship is made the richer by the infinite variety of thy creation; and for each child and man and woman in this church we give thee thanks and praise.

We thank thee for those whose eyes were long since lifted to thy face and who have found their peace long since in the vision of thy glory. Upon thine altar we place their gifts of time and talent, their offerings of planning and striving; and we pray that thou wilt confirm in them thy pledge that they who lose their lives for thy sake shall find them again as otherwise they never could have found them.

We thank thee for those whose loyalty is not yet brought to flame, those who sit and watch but do not put their shoulders to a wheel nor help to push the heavy load along the upward way, those who bear within themselves the means of victory and joy but never understand what hope their selfhood embraces. Let some word or thought lodge fast within their minds, we pray. Strike fire within their souls; awaken them from slumber; commit their wills to noble purposes; and spare them, Lord, the charge that inasmuch as they did it not for those whom thou dost love, they did it not for thee.

We pray for those now lifted from our ranks by illness or age. We prize their courage and their patience, and we cherish as a valued contribution to our fellowship their steadfastness in pain of body or of mind, in weariness, monotony, and fear. Grant them to know that thou still holdest them in thy care, givest them the strength by which they daily live, and in thy providence findest use for what they are and say and do.

For all our fellows in this church we pray and give thee thanks, our Father, and we beseech thee that all may so entrust themselves to thee that thou canst find a place of trust for them. Through Jesus Christ our Lord. *Amen.*

## Who share our home

O thou who hast set us down in a world where multitudes of men and women share our common earthly home, and who hast ordained that our neighbors hold in their hands the power to cast us into grief or lead us into joy, we pray for those whose lives have touched our own.

There are some that are good. We like them, and with them we find it easy to live in the peace which thou didst plan for all thy children. Grant us to bless thee day by day for the providence which brought them forth in the hour of their birth, for the graciousness which they have earned by their mercy and patience, and for the privilege which we enjoy in their friendship. Guide us to open our hearts to them and in the comradeship of work and play to find a foretaste of thy heavenly kingdom.

But there are also some who are bad. They have grievously sinned; and, stained and warped and broken, they beget in our hearts only shame and disgust. They are selfish, lustful, small of mind, and mean of purpose, and seeing them, we never look without dismay. Yet we would not rest content in our distaste, our Father, and we pray that thou wilt restrain us from judging lest we ourselves be judged. Illumine the selfishness within our own souls—the lust, the smallness of mind, and the meanness of purpose. Give us toward others that same compassion which thou hast always held toward ourselves, and chasten us until we pray in good faith: "Forgive us our sins as we forgive those who have sinned against us."

And then there are some whom we simply do not like. They intend us no harm; they have done us no wrong; they have committed no sin that we could name or condemn. But we are jealous of their successes; we rejoice in their failures; and we long to see them out of favor with their fellows. Broaden our hearts, we beseech thee, that we may be glad in the very diversity which now repels us. Help us to find in people different from ourselves thy chance to do thy will in ways beyond our own power to assist thee, and spur us to see in their strangeness not unsightliness and disdain but wonder and praise.

Thou hast made of thy children a family. Thou hast so ordered thy world that none can do good without blessing his fellows, nor any do ill without harming the people around him. Forgive us, we pray, the wrong that we have done our brothers without knowing we did it, and forgive us even more the wrong that we have done, knowing full well what we did. Through Jesus Christ our Lord. *Amen.*

## SPECIAL OCCASIONS

*First Sunday in Advent*

Almighty God, Father of our Lord Jesus Christ and Holy Spirit loving all that thou hast made, prepare us, we pray, for the hours when we shall celebrate the birth of thy Son. The world is so much with us, and its allurements are so steadily before us. We long to save this Christmas for thy purposes, but so frequently our good intentions have lost their way in the forests of dinners and parties, in the jungles of buying and wrapping. So we beseech thee to loose us fom the bondage of our long-established habits and in this time of the Advent to fix our minds on him whose coming we proclaim.

Let these be days of judgment, our Father—days when we remember thy creation of the world and thy decision that it was good, days when our hearts encircle all its distant reaches and comprehend the cruelty which man has worked upon his brother man, days when we understand our own responsibility for the wickedness that brings thee pain. Grant that our heads may not rest easy on pillows bought with greed or injustice, and be thou the end of any peace that has no better source than ignorance, indifference, or such enchantment with our own concerns that we have no leisure for the agonies around us. Deny us success when we try to forget that men are starving—now, that men are homeless—now, that men are persecuted—now; and if we hail the coming of thy Son, let it not be without the awareness that inasmuch as we have not done the deeds of righteousness to one of the least of thy creatures, we have not done them unto thy Son.

But vouchsafe that these may also be days of joy, our Father—days when we recall that the Word became flesh when flesh had no right to expect it, days when we recognize anew that thou dost love thy people less because of their merits than in spite of their unworthiness, days when we find in the life and death of Jesus the evidence of thine unflagging toil for our redemption. If thou didst care enough for the world to give thine only begotten Son that whosoever believed on him might have abundant life, protect us from the insolence of despising what thou dost love. If the earth is thine and its people are thy creatures, save us from the folly of believing that thou hast lost control of thy creation. If thou hast kept thy favor for the righteous and laid in a manger thy gift above all other gifts, deliver us from the fear that the horses of history no longer respond to thy reins.

Make us ready for Christmas, God. By peace or by strife, by joy or by anguish, by life or by death—prepare us for the holy day of incarnation, and when thou art praised for the birth of thy Son, may it be by men and women born again in him whose birth they sing. Through Jesus Christ our Lord. *Amen.*

## Second Sunday in Advent

God of power and God of love, who didst send before thy Son a host of witnesses and herald his coming with prophets foretelling his glory, we thank thee that Christmas does not burst upon us unannounced. For the weeks to make ready and the days to prepare, we bless thee, our Father. For the call to repent and the time to be forgiven, we bless thee, our Father; and we pray that when the joyous hour has come to hail again the birth of our Lord, we may not stand before the manger unequipped for what we see.

If ever our souls have magnified thy holy name or our spirits rejoiced in thy salvation, let them praise and glorify thee now. How can we look upon so much and understand so little, how hear the words of everlasting life but turn away as if they had no meaning, how live in daily debt to thy beneficence yet speak as if we condescended to acknowledge thine existence? Thou who art mighty hast done great things for us, and from generation to generation thy mercy is on those who fear thee. Thou hast shown strength with thine arm, scattered the proud in the imagination of their hearts, put down the mighty from their thrones, and exalted those of low degree. Thou hast filled the hungry with good things, and the rich thou hast sent empty away. In remembrance of thy mercy thou hast helped thy servants, and as thou didst speak to our fathers, so hast thou spoken to their posterity forever.

Make us aware, O Lord. Make us aware of thy goodness to us and to all mankind. Deepen our consciousness that thy love surrounds us like the air that we breathe, that thy power sustains us like the ground on which we walk, that thy light leads us like the stars in the sky and the road signs on the highway. Chasten our pride, but increase our self-respect. Show us our sins, but destroy not our hope. Teach us how completely we depend upon thy grace, but fill us with the eagerness to serve thee as we can. And grant that, kneeling before we stand, waiting before we run, and forgiving before we ask forgiveness, we may come at last to Christmas in the humble strength of those who have accepted their weakness. Through Jesus Christ our Lord. *Amen.*

## Third Sunday in Advent

O thou in whom we live and move and have our being, King of kings and Lord of lords, God of the ages past and Ruler of all that is or evermore shall be, we lift our hearts to thee in these days of penitence and preparation, and we bless thee for the holy memories that cluster about them. Once and long ago thou didst send thy Son to Bethlehem's far hills: send him now again, we pray, and through his ministry among us let thy kingdom come, thy will be done.

To those who bring their brothers pain and want and fear, to those who see the truth but turn their backs upon it, to those who kill and steal and maim—to these and all men more who flaunt thy purposes, let Christ be as a burning fire to gather up their sin and thrust it from the world which thou hast made. To those whose eyes are blind to that which thou didst intend man's life to be, to those who yearn for faith but find in their souls not trust but fear, to those long blessed with all the good which thou canst give but burdened so with all their riches that they cannot climb the steep and narrow way—to these and all men more who hunger and thirst after righteousness but seek in vain the food and drink which thou dost provide, let Christ be as the Way and the Truth and the Life, a beacon on lofty mountains, a window on far horizons, a light in darkened skies.

Send us thy Christ again as each has need of him and thee, and grant us grace to open our hearts at his coming. As once from lonely fields the shepherds sped to see the child in manger hay, may we hasten from highway and byway, from office and home, from school and store, and kneel in quietness before thy gift divine. As Wise Men swiftly crossed the moors and mountains seeking peace and hope in thee, may we see thy star and swiftly follow, resting not until it stands above some new revealing of thy will and way.

Show us thy Word made flesh, we beseech thee, until in him born long since and far away we see the very image of thyself, thy Spirit cloaked in manhood, thy purpose wrought incarnate, thy heavens opened and thy glory bared to mortal eyes. We are thy children, Lord: make us then thy prophets, that we may tell on the earth the glad tidings of our Father in heaven. We are thy disciples, Lord: make us then thy witnesses, that we may proclaim to all mankind what is the height and depth and breadth of thy love, which thou didst once reveal to men in Jesus Christ our Lord. *Amen.*

## Fourth Sunday in Advent

Eternal God, who dost love us even when we are unlovable and believe in us long after we have lost belief in thee, we bless thee for the word of hope that whispers through the tinseled glitter by which we choose to celebrate the advent of thy Son. We praise thee that the years have not been able quite to silence those who tell again the wondrous story of thy love for men which shone anew when Christ was born at Bethlehem. We thank thee that if Christmas means shopping and parties; if Christmas means ornamented trees and lighted windows; if Christmas means Santa Claus and Yule logs and wassail bowls—Christmas first means Christ.

Grant, Lord, that each of us may find the deeper meanings of these days before the Christmastide. Lead us to see afresh thy patience, thy humility, and thy never-fainting goodness. Restore in us the knowledge of our creaturehood, our blindness and our sin, and as we stand unworthy in thy presence, receive us not because of what we are but in spite of it.

Let our hearts be warm in these days, our Father, and from their hearthfires let not the humblest soul be turned away. If we have wronged a brother, vouchsafe that this may be the time when we ask his forgiveness. If we have failed to serve thee where we had the strength and opportunity, make these the hours when we cast aside our lethargy or fear. If we have kept apart from thee and, daily drawing life from thy love, yet lived as if thou wert an idle dream, so touch these moments spent in thy praise that before we turn toward home again, we lift an honest prayer to thee and seek thy grace and wait thy will.

Through all the darkened skies of earth still send

thy star to go before us. Lead us, like eager men of long ago, until at last we find ourselves before some stable door of unexpected import, and grant that entering to worship, we may not depart except to bear new burdens in thy name. Through Jesus Christ our Lord. *Amen.*

## Christmas

O thou who wast of old where shepherds watched their flocks by night and angels sang their songs of praise around the babe of Bethlehem, we turn to thee as Christmas comes again to earth, and we seek thy star as long ago the Wise Men rode their camels toward the stable of the inn. Dark the days are now, our Father, as the days were dark where Joseph lived with Mary, and earth has need of thee today no less than it had need of thee when Herod sat upon his throne in Palestine. For once again we beat the plowshares into swords and into spears the pruning hooks, and what might be the building stones of peace become instead the missiles of destruction. We have wandered from thy will, and searching for the place where Christ is born today, we have not found a better highway than the broken roads on which the generations found despair before us.

Open thou for us, O Lord, the gates which we have not swung wide to thee ourselves. Take away the pride which does not let us see our need of thee. Strip off the vain pretensions by which we convince ourselves that we can save ourselves. Confront us with thy wisdom and thy love, and, coming thus as close to thee as mortal man may come, may we have the sense to kneel as did the kings who came to Bethlehem.

Encourage in us once again the simple virtues of our fathers in the faith. Defend us from believing that sophistication is a sign of excellence, or power always proof of goodness, or popularity an evidence of truth or righteousness. Make us teachable again, open-minded, and sure enough about the sins which we have done ourselves to be forgiving of the sins committed by our fellows. Give us the earnestness of those who think that everything depends upon the effort which they spend themselves, and yet the calmness of those who know that thou art Lord of all, that nothing can defeat thee, and that though all else change and pass away, thou dost not change through all eternity.

For the sick and the sorrowing, for the hurt and the hurried, for the lost and the lonely, we lift a special prayer this day. Through the open doors of thy love bring each of them, our Father, and be to each of them the light that never fails. And so may all the world acknowledge thee as King, until at last peace reigns upon the earth and good will never leaves the hearts of men. Through Jesus Christ our Lord. *Amen.*

## Sunday after Christmas

Thou art so still in thine approach to us, our Father. Thou art so quiet and so humble. Thou comest, and we do not know that thou hast come. Thou sustainest us, and we do not recognize the source of our sustenance. We touch thy works and call them "nature," and we see thy might and call it "evolution," and living in the midst of thee, we say we cannot find thee.

Yet being blind to thee, we long to banish our need to cherish our blindness, and we pray that thou wilt so cross the borders of our fragile dominions that we find thee at last a Lord who cannot be ignored. Help us to find thee in the common happenings of daily living—in babies born at home or hospital and bringing with their birth fresh hope for a worn and wearied earth, in the companionship of home and family where man and woman share their holy ties with one another in their partnership with thee, in the nearness of associates at work and competitors in business, in words spoken to neighbors and deeds done for friends and hands stretched out to bridge the seas to lay their benediction on the starving and homeless. Thou hast said through Christ that what we do to one of the least of thy creatures we do no less to thee, and we pray that thou wilt lead us to seek thee where thou canst be found—in the mansions where the mighty live without ever understanding that the earth belongs to none but thee, and in the hovels of the poor who have not seen their riches in the things the world can never take away; in men who pride themselves on peace which thou regardest as their condemnation, and in those who suffer pain from which no skill of man can save them; in the lonely toilers of

*105*

kitchen and schoolroom, in the unsupported prophets of town hall and court, in the solitary pilgrims of office and store.

Like shepherds in the fields abiding, grant that we may hear the angels sing where day meets day in endless tasks and tired chores; and shouldst thou bless us with a breathless moment at some new-created manger, spare us the judgment that we looked but did not see. Like Wise Men riding from a distant land to stand beneath the star and loose their gifts of gold and frankincense and myrrh, grant us, too, the wisdom to forsake the far countries where we have wasted our worship on gods that had no right to it, and to bend our knees in this Christmastide to none except thy Son.

Let thy peace be in our hearts, our Father, and let thy power dwell within us, too. Let thy blessing rest upon us, but teach us also how to bring thy blessing to a world that does not know it needs it. Through Jesus Christ our Lord. *Amen.*


## New Year's Day

This day we stand, O Lord, upon the ridge between the years; and looking backward, we see the days that are gone, and, looking forward, the days that yet must come. For all that thou hast given us of old we speak our thanks to thee—for the sunny hours in which we had no doubts about thy mercy but also for those darker moments when we learned the price which thou didst pay to make us as we are. And for the days that lie ahead of us we speak our thanks to thee—for the hope of good in time to come, for the chance to work for righteousness, and for the faith that thou wilt ever walk beside us as we go.

We speak, our Father, but still there is so much unspoken in our hearts. Hear then the prayers that none can know save thee and him from whom they rise—the prayer for the well-beloved son in military service overseas, for the dear one lying ill at home, for the strength to bear the burdens which the dawning week will bring, for pardon in the things which we have done but know we should have left undone, for bridles to control our anger and reins to handle our fears and brakes to slow our blinded pride. Whatever the prayer in whatever the heart, thou knowest, and each for all and all for each, we ask that thou wilt so respond to our petitions that through each of us and all of us thy saving health may be among us.

Convince us anew of thy love and thy power, and as the mountains rise above the plains around them, grant that we may stand unmoved among the anxieties and cares that now beset us. Keep us alike from being fretful in the things we cannot change and heedless of the things we can. Save us from the trembling of those who have forgotten thy part in the world's redemption but also from the complacency of those who have forgotten their own. Help us as we try to discover where we came from, who we are, and why we are here; and vouchsafe that by the leading of thy grace we may make each day a contribution to thy purpose. Show us the

ways that end in peace, the paths that point to righteousness, the trails that take the heart to never-failing
love; and giving us the substance of courage, defend us
from the temptation to be false. Teach us so to be free
that our liberty may not become our bondage and that,
bound to thy will, we may be strong for thy service. Let
this year bring joy to thy kingdom, and to thee be the
honor, to thee the glory, and to thee the praise. Through
Jesus Christ our Lord. *Amen.*

## Epiphany

God of all holiness and power, who wast not content to give thy Son only to thy chosen people Israel
but didst send a star and led the Gentile kings to stand
before the manger with the Jewish shepherds, we praise
thy name for men of every race and creed and land. We
thank thee that thou didst shine in our hearts to give the
light of the knowledge of thy glory in the face of Jesus
Christ, and we pray for ourselves for the sake of our
brothers.

From the peace that rests at ease with what has
ever been and does not strive toward higher heights beyond, save us, our Father. From the fear that hides its
weakness in cruelty and obscures its doubt with pre-
tense, save us, our Father. From the easy way that finds
its victories in words and never asks that words be
shaped to deeds, save us, our Father. From such pride
in our own strength that we do not lean on thee and

from such skill in falsehood that we do not seek the truth, save us, our Father. And where already we have sinned, forgive us, chasten us, redeem us.

Thou dost love all of thy children with an everlasting love and feel the hurt of each as if it were thine own, and we call to thy tender remembrance all thy people who suffer pain or hardship because of man's inhumanity to man. We pray for those who have no food to eat or clothes to wear or homes to shelter them from wind and cold. Surround them with thy mercy and protect them by thy power; and stir our will to aid them in their helplessness. We pray for those who are persecuted because of the color of their skin or the land of their birth or the creed of their allegiance. Encircle them with thy love and defend them by thy might; and quicken our desire to be their brothers in the household of thy care. We pray for those who bear their neighbors' burdens—doctors and nurses whose healing ministry is less the means of livelihood than a way to merit life, teachers who find the truth a gospel and in the gospel find the truth, laborers whose toil is not the drudgery of slaves but the privilege of men who share thy purpose, leaders of the nations who see in their power not an opportunity to be served but to serve.

Let thy star shine again in the darkness, Lord. Grant that it may bring to the manger all races and peoples, and in the offering of their manifold gifts, let the glory of thy Son be manifest through every land of earth. In Jesus' name. *Amen.*

## Brotherhood Sunday

God of all nations and peoples, Lord of all places and lands, who didst form man of the dust of the ground, and breathe into his nostrils the breath of life, and make of him a living soul, we praise thee for the infinite variety of thy human creatures. We thank thee for the wonderful shadings of color and shape, the incredible differences of insight and habit, and especially the endless flights of heart and mind that lift thy children above the beasts of the field and let them share a holy comradeship with thee. Glory be to thee for thy creation of man! Glory be to thee for his manifold diversities!

Yet even as we magnify thy name, we seek thy forgiveness; for we have sinned against our brothers and done evil in thy sight. We have looked on the outward appearance and not on the heart, passed judgment in terms of what men had and not of what they were, called ourselves thy sons but lived as if we thought all other men our slaves. We have seen pain without pity and heard of want without compassion. We have despised our brothers for their ignorance but denied them the means of knowledge, forced them to fight for what they needed but condemned their aggressiveness, offered them no opportunities except servitude but complained because they were nothing but servants. We have withheld our neighbors' rights and thought we had the right to withhold them, and we have hated thy creatures without understanding that we were hating their Creator. Forgive us, we pray. Forgive us.

Save us from the insecurity that makes us fearful, and free us from the fear that leads to arrogance. Teach us whence we came, who we are, and whither we shall go; and grant that, proud to be thy sons and daughters, we may need no other cause for pride. If we have beaten our plowshares into swords and our pruning hooks into spears, give us grace to shape our swords to plowshares and our spears to pruning hooks. Deepen the roots of our faith. Widen the circle of our love. And help us so to live with all our brothers on the earth that thou wilt have a place for us among them in thy realm of many mansions. Through Jesus Christ our Lord. *Amen.*

## Ash Wednesday

How many, O Lord, are the sins which we have committed against thy love! How manifold is our need of thy pardon! When we remember thy great goodness, our hearts are heavy within us; for thou didst create us in thine own image, and now we bear upon ourselves so little likeness of the Father who begot us.

Thou dost love even the unlovable, but we have never hated men more surely than when they did not hold our hatefulness against us. Thou dost deal justly even with injustice, but we have never found integrity more difficult than when honest men most merited our honesty. Patient, thou hast found us hasty; pure, thou knowest our corruption; steadfast, thou bearest the hardships of our fickleness; tolerant, thou needest no herald to tell thee of our arrogance.

*111*

Hear us as we make our confession to thee. Forgive us both the sins which we have recognized and repented and also the sins which we have repented but not recognized. And renew a right spirit within us that we may henceforth live in probity and evermore seek only the straight, clean path of thy love.

Keep us from being so insecure that we hide our fearfulness behind a wall of petulance. Save us from the frustrations that vent their disappointment with ourselves on those with whom we have no reason to be disappointed. Shield us from spending all our pleasantries on acquaintances and reserving only ugliness for relatives. Thwart us when we try to stand high by standing on our brothers, and if we have borne false witness against our neighbors, give us no peace until we understand the truth about ourselves.

We pray not that the way may be smooth nor the burdens light. We ask not to be sheltered from thy judgment on the fearful choices we must make. But do thou cleanse our hearts of the stain of their iniquity, and open our eyes to the counsels of thine eternal wisdom, and set our hands to the deeds of thy mercy. For we would be good, our Father—good not that we may reap the rewards of thy favor, but good that we may serve thy will, good that we may give the world joy and not sorrow, good that when at last thou dost remove us from our earthly home, we may stand before thy throne as faithful followers of Jesus Christ our Lord. *Amen.*

## Palm Sunday

O thou who art the Father of our Lord Jesus Christ and who didst look with a father's eye on that day when he rode into the Holy City of old, we sound his praises now as once the people raised their shouts beside the crowded way. "Hosanna!" we cry. "Hosanna in the highest! Blessed is he that cometh in the name of the Lord!" For the courage that held him fast along the stony way, for the confidence that kept command of fear, for the knowledge of thee that left him not alone— we give our gratitude to thee, who art the author of every good and perfect gift. Upon the lanes of our minds we lay down our garments before him, and we wave palm branches to the Son whom thou didst send that we might have life and have it more abundantly.

Yet we remember, our Father, how soon "Hosanna!" turned to "Crucify!" With the bright hope of this day blind not our eyes to the wickedness that lies within. Save us from the luxury of joy when we have not earned the right to be joyful. Spare us the judgment that on Sunday we hailed thy Son in glory and on Friday nailed him to the cross in shame.

Thou knowest how often the burden of bewilderment lies heavy upon us. Thou seest how hard is the fulfillment of faith in our hearts. Thou understandest how we want to love thee perfectly and to serve thee with all our might, but how readily still we turn from the lengthening road because our marching wearies both our faith and our feet. Pierce then the shadowed skies that fend thy light away. Make known thyself to us as once thou didst to Moses in the days long gone, until we see that though the fires of hatred roar around thee, thou art not consumed. Come thou to us as once thou didst to Isaiah in the temple, until above the shouts of wicked men we see thee high and lifted up, Creator of our life and Master of our ways. Speak thou to us as once thou didst to Christ within the darkness of the quiet garden hill, until we take the cup which thou dost give and in the sorrow and the pain find peace and rest.

We give ourselves to thee, our Father, and in thy love we have no fear. For thine is the will that grows not weary; thine is the mind that thinks no wrong; thine is the heart that circles all thy children; thine is the kingdom, and thine the power, and thine the glory. Through Jesus Christ our Lord. *Amen.*

## Maundy Thursday

Almighty and eternal God, whose rule is over all and who understandest our thoughts before we speak them unto thee, we turn to thee in prayer because we know our need of thee and because we hunger for the fellowship which thou dost freely offer those who seek thy strength and light. We strain our minds to think thy thoughts after thee, discover how thou hast decreed that men were meant to live together on the earth, see our way more clearly through the fog that fills the onward road. Yet when we consider thy heavens, the work of thy fingers, the moon and the stars which thou hast ordained, we bow again with him who asked of thee, "What is man that thou art mindful of him, or the son of man that thou visitest him?"—and when we seek to compass the world that thou hast made, we walk once more with him who said, "Such knowledge is too wonderful for me. It is high. I cannot attain unto it."

To forge a just and lasting peace among the nations of the earth, to end the strife of management and labor, to burn away the hatreds that keep the races separate, to root out the evil of our own hearts and minds—Lord, we have tried to do these things and failed. Our minds are too weak. Our hearts are too small. So we turn to thee like him who sought thee on that night of old when his sweat was as great drops of blood falling down upon the ground, and again we say we need thee. More even than we know, we need thee.

Be to us now what once thou wast to our fathers—a rock and a refuge, a very present help in trouble; a light and salvation, a God in whom to have no fear. Lift us to hilltops, we pray, and show us, far beyond the present night, the day toward which thy purpose leads. Then send us out again upon the highways, and when the roads divide before us, guide thou our feet lest they wander or grow weary. Help us to love thee with all our heart and mind, all our soul and strength, until we have no will but thine and ask no joy but that of serving thee. Help us to love our neighbors as ourselves, until no goad of pride or spur of greed can thrust us into conflict with thy grace. Keep us steadfast in our own

*115*

Gethsemane, and if we dread what man can do on Golgotha, make us glad in what thou hast already done in Joseph's garden. Through Jesus Christ our Lord. *Amen.*

## Good Friday

God of grace and glory, who didst love thy Son too much to shield him from the need to love, we praise thee for the revelation of thyself in Jesus Christ. In him thou hast made thyself known to thy people, and before the patience of thy mercy and the meekness of thy power we stand in awe and adoration, seeing only in part but filled with gratitude for the part that we see.

Touch the heart of each of us in this hour, Lord. Thou knowest us far better even than we know ourselves, and what we need is thine to give and thine alone. Through silence, song, and spoken word be present among us, we pray, and those blessings which we can neither give ourselves nor take from thee against thy will, grant us for the sake of those to whom we pledge them in thy name.

The strong among us, the men and women sound of body and alert in mind whose dedicated influence could make thy will incarnate—confirm them in their strength, our Father, and lead them so to use it that they may do good and not evil through all of their days on the earth. The weak among us, the people of humble station and few talents, of feeble flesh and troubled hearts, who must ever add their own infirmities to any other burden thrust upon them—comfort them in their frailty, our Father, and teach them that thou canst use their weakness to magnify thy power. The disillusioned among us, the questing souls who want to believe but cannot and who hunger for faith but have not found it —save them from pride in their disillusionment, our Father, and keep them on the searching road until the darkness disappears and the memory of the night makes them prophets of the day.

Help us to take up our own crosses—not the illnesses and accidents which we could neither foresee nor avoid, not the burdens and responsibilities which rightly fall to our province of duty, but the tasks for which we could never be conscripted, the service to which we could never be commanded, the toil for whose neglect we could never be censured. Help us to feel as if they were our own the hunger of the starving and the cold of the homeless, the bitterness of those who have no freedom and the fear of those who have no hope, the pain of the young who have not found a cause to merit their devotion and the despair of the old who watch in helplessness the torment of their children's indecision. Save us from contentment in security which we deserve no more than hosts of other men who do not have it, and defend us from assuming that our privilege of birth or circumstance is evidence of special favor in thy sight.

If we have been asleep through agonies we might have spared our brothers, stab us awake. Let thy kingdom come in us, thy will be done in us; and in the cross of thy Son vouchsafe that we may find our peace and strength for life and death. *Amen.*

## Easter

God of all power and love, who didst lift from the grave our Lord Jesus Christ and by thy mighty power bring him to the life that knows no end, we praise thee that, being often dead while still alive, we yet may be alive in spite of death. We have come to thy house burdened with the knowledge of our own sin, sick with the wretchedness that we have seen all around us, and weary with the vain attempt to leave a decent heritage behind us. We have beheld thy glory, but always through a glass and darkly. We have heard thy word, but seldom clear enough to leave no doubt it came from thee. Day by day the crosses mark the circling skies, and none need prove to us that pain exists or that unrighteousness is strong; but standing by the empty tomb, we scarcely dare investigate its emptiness, fearing to know lest, having known, we wish that we had been content with ignorance.

Come to us in this hour, O God. Whether we expect thee or sit in utter confidence that thou art not to be expected; whether we recognize thee or, having met thee, say that we have never seen thee; whether we deserve thy favor or merit only thy disdain—come to us in this hour, and do for us what we have not been able to do for ourselves. Descend upon us in thy pure and holy spirit. Cleanse us of the evil that leaves us unmoved by thy love. Free us from the hardness of heart that sees a brother crushed but does not lift his load. We believe in thee: help thou our unbelief. Disturb our confident assumptions; shatter our stubborn complacency; burn away our ugly pretensions; and stand us on our feet again as men and women created in thine own image and bearing on themselves the likeness of thyself.

We fear the wickedness without, our Father, but even more, we fear the weakness within; and praying that thou wilt save us from the world, we pray with still greater earnestness that thou wilt save us from ourselves. Raise us from the graves of our own digging. Loose us from the tombs of our own building. Redeem us from the sins which can be laid upon no conscience other than our own. Let this be indeed a day of earthquake and thick darkness—a day when the careless foundations of our lives are shaken down to firmness, a day when the winds of thy wrath blow out the boasted lamps of man and force upon us the awareness that our proud sufficiency is insufficient. Yet, too, let this be a day of rejoicing and great gladness—a day when suddenly we understand that although with men the saving of man is impossible, with thee all things are possible; a day when thou dost surprise us with the insight that in our weakness thou canst make perfect thy strength and through the foolishness of the cross reveal thy wisdom and power. In Jesus' name. *Amen.*

## Family Sunday

O thou who hast revealed to us in Christ the life thou didst intend for us, and offered us in him the power and the peace to be as thou wouldst have us be, we call to thy remembrance the homes from which we come and back to which we soon shall go. For all the good that we have known in them we give the thanks to thee, since thou didst first ordain that man should dwell in families, and thou didst bring to being those we love beyond all others on the earth. For all the wrong that we have done in them, we ask thy pardon and correction, since our sin is not against ourselves but thee, and though we strive as if we were a hundred men, we still are blind unless we have the guidance of thy grace.

Be thou in all the homes here represented. Where love is, and lovingkindness, where peace and all the blessed fruits of peacefulness, where self-denial and the will to set the other's good above his own—be thou known to all who dwell within the house, and by thy presence fix them fast upon the heights and keep them steadfast evermore.

But be thou none the less in other homes, we pray, and if it be that some are here from homes in which the light of love has been extinguished, grant these the purity to find again the kindling spark of faith and right decision. Drive out the bitterness, O God. Drive out the hatred. Help us to be at peace within ourselves and hence to live more readily in peace with those who share our dwelling place. Give us grace to put unnecessary pride behind us and not to try so much to have our own wills done as to make our homes a healthy cell within the living body of thy kingdom. Bridge thou the gulf between the generations, and let the elderly do honor to the vigor of the young and the youthful seek eagerly the wisdom of the old. Save us embarrassment in speaking of thy will to those we love best, and empower us to fashion homes where thou art mentioned often and thy purpose held the end of all their being.

Be thou, too, in homes that hold an empty chair. Touch the memories of those who live alone, and while they call to mind again the faces of the ones they loved of old, confirm them in their faith that one day soul shall meet again beloved soul, and partings be no more.

Take then these homes of ours, Lord. Take them, and make them wholly thine, till every house sing forth thy praise and every family proclaim the good, glad word of Jesus Christ our Lord. *Amen.*

*Pentecost*

Eternal God, who art the Father of all men and all peoples, the Lord of all ages and lands, we thank thee for the church of Jesus Christ thy Son. We remember thy promise in him that where two or three were gathered together in his name, there wouldst thou be in their midst, and we praise thee that thou hast ever kept thy covenant and dwelt in love with those who loved to dwell with thee. For the prophets of old who have spoken thy word and claimed neither increase nor ease, for the saints of the years who have been to thee as the hands and the feet of thy mercy, for the ageless multitudes of the humble whose stature is small in the mind of the world but whose names are writ large in the book of thy love, for the martyr bands who had no gift more dear than life but counted life a gift too dear for any Lord but thyself—for these and all men else who kept the faith in fellowship and found in fellowship the freedom to be faithful, we speak our gratitude to thee, and we bless thee for the fathers who begot us.

Descend upon us now as first thou didst upon the church beyond the seas, and let not Pentecost depart while we still sit cold before thee. Breathe once more thy breath of power. Send again thy tongues of fire. Fill today the house with glory.

In shame we confess that we have often sought thy kingdom only when all other realms had turned us away; that saying we would gladly die for thee, we have not been willing even to live for thee; and that thinking we were seeking thee, we have fled from thy presence lest thou shouldst ask of us a greater gift than we loved thee enough to bestow. Yet we know that thou art life, that apart from thee is only death, and that thou art nowhere found more surely than where thy people meet to serve thee. So we pray that thou wilt permit us no escape from the fellowship of those who believe, neither cleave us from the army of the loyal souls who fight for thee on daily battlefields of home and neighborhood, of school and marketplace. Make us again thy body in the church—thy lips to speak thy gospel, thy hands to bear thy burdens, thine eyes to see man's anguish, thy feet to bear thy healing ministry to all who stand in need of it. And to thee be the glory for ever and ever. *Amen.*

## Memorial Day

God of all power and glory, who wast and art and art to come, before whom the generations rise and pass away, to whose mercy there is no limit and of whose providence no end, we turn to thee as people standing in the need of thee, and we seek thy help because we know that thou art all the strength we have.

This day our thoughts turn back along the trail of time, and especially we think of those whose faithfulness and sacrifice still keep alive their benediction among us. We thank thee for thy servants, the prophets and martyrs who, being afraid of none but thee, have spoken unafraid the words of justice and scorned to let timidity deny the claims of righteousness. We thank thee for the mighty men of every age and land who found their might no cause for either indolence or ruthlessness, and we thank thee no less for men of little strength who trusted that thou couldst use even their weakness, and humbly laid upon thine altars what they had. For all who walked with thee in truth and love we bless thee, Lord, and we pray that thou wilt ever nourish within us the memory of those who kept the faith of old.

Hear us, too, we beseech thee, as we call to thy remembrance the well-beloved souls with whom we once were bound in closest fellowship. Silently we name them in our hearts—father or mother, son or daughter, brother or sister or stanchly loyal friend. Silently we live again the life we lived with them on earth, know once more the love we had for them, feel anew our sorrow in their going from us, and most of all declare the warmth in which we hold them still. Thy universe is big, our Father, and thy ways are past our comprehension, but whithersoever they have gone in thy wide worlds of providence and lovingkindness, be thou with them to comfort and uphold. We pray for them, thrust out our minds toward them, cry out to them that we have not forgotten, and, asking their forgiveness for the wrong we did to them, bless them for the joy they brought us by their daily words and deeds.

Grant that as we think about these loved ones now departed, we may neither dwell too long upon the past nor deal lightly with the lessons of the days that are gone. Save us from assuming that homage is a substitute for service. Teach us that victory was won no easier of old than now, and that now no more than then is courage reached without persistence or goodness gained without labor. Thou hast blessed us with a gallant heritage: bless us now with hope and faithfulness. Through Jesus Christ our Lord. *Amen.*

## Children's Day

Everlasting God, thou whom our fathers have known through the years, and our grandfathers, and all the hosts of other men who walked the earth for centuries before we ever saw the light of day ourselves, we quiet our minds, and we calm our souls, and we ask that we may know thee, too. Thou understandest how we long for thee, how we wish that we might see thee as we see our friends, touch thee as we touch a piece of stone or wood or clay, hear thee as we hear the notes of the organ or the voices of the choir. Thou understandest also how many times we think thee far away, how many times we even wonder whether a being like thee exists at all. So we turn to thee now and ask that thou wilt help us in our struggle after faith.

Grant us to see that thy handiwork is all around us —in the blue sky and the white clouds of a lazy summer afternoon, in the sun by day and the moon and stars by night, in the falling snow of winter storms and the grass and flowers of the springtime. Teach us to find a witness to thy presence in the people whom we meet along the way—in father and mother, brother and sister, friend and foe. Thou didst create each one of them, O Lord, and through them thy Holy Spirit shines, sometimes dim and sometimes clear, but ever speaking to our hearts of thee from whom they came. And then lead us to recognize thee in the history of nations and lands—in the battle of the right and the wrong, in the conflict of the good and the bad, in the long, long quest to find a way to peace and brotherhood.

Thou knowest, our Father, how we yearn to do the right: be thou our guide to keep us on the upward path. Thou knowest how we want to be brave: strengthen our

125

hearts and save us from fear of other people, fear of failure, fear of ourselves. Thou knowest how we strive to serve thee faithfully: be thou the light to lure us through the host of lesser loyalties that seek our wills. So shall we at last be truly friends of thine, followers of Christ, and ministers of thy purpose for the world. In Jesus' name. *Amen.*

## Independence Day

God of all power and mercy, from whom no prayer escapes unnoticed, we have come to thy house together, but we seek thee one by one. Stoop then to the prayers we raise from hearts that know their need of thee, and through the silence let the voice of our longing be heard.

Let each of us thank God for the world in which we live—the majesty of its mountains, the quiet of its woodlands, the wideness of its oceans, the glory of its skies, the richness of its fruited plains and amber waves of grain. Let each of us thank God for the world in which we live. [*Silent prayer.*]

Let each of us thank God for this land we love beyond all other lands—its heritage in righteousness and justice, its ancestry in truth and freedom, its wealth and power, its comfort and security, its opportunity and hope. Let each of us thank God for this land we love beyond all other lands. [*Silent prayer.*]

Let us confess to God the part that we have had in the sins of our nation—the greed that claimed for ourselves what we denied to our brothers, the fear that bred prejudice and the prejudice that fostered hatred, the might that made us callous and the peace that left us blind, the liberty that turned to license, and the safety that became a soporific, and the affluence that lured us into arrogance. Let us confess to God the part that we have had in the sins of our nation, and let us ask his forgiveness. [*Silent prayer.*]

Let us pray that God will match our nation to his need of her—that standing unafraid before the threat of man, she may kneel unashamed in the presence of her Lord; that the troubled may find in her solace, the hungry food, and the homeless a home; that free, she may be free to love mercy, that strong, she may be strong for the right, and that wise, she may be wise enough to understand her ignorance. [*Silent prayer.*]

O thou who hast a care for all lands and all peoples, save us, we beseech thee, from making this nation a haven for preferments of race or distinctions of class. Spare us the sin of turning our backs on the family of other nations. Establish us within the fellowship that has no exiles, and when we try to come to thee alone, deny us thy blessing until our brothers stand beside us. Through Jesus Christ our Lord. *Amen.*

## Labor Day

Almighty and eternal God, who lovest none of thy children more than another and who holdest each in thy care as if he were thine only begotten, we come to thee together that each may come to thee alone. From vastly different tasks we have entered thy house this day, and back to widely varied ways we soon shall go. Thou hast called some of us to be keepers of stores, some to be mothers and housewives, some to be teachers or students, some to be secretaries or salesmen or toilers with wood and brick and stone; and we pray that thou wilt so lengthen our sight that we may henceforth find thee daily in the daily labor of our minds and hands.

Grant us to know that thou hast a need for us no less than thy need of the priests and the prophets of old; that when our work is done in thy name, we stand on holy ground to do it; and that thou willest more that men should serve their fellows than that they should only speak of serving. Through Christ thou hast taught us to pray for our daily bread: show us through him how great is thy care for every hour any man spends on the earth, for the food that he eats and the clothes that he wears, for his joy and his pain, for his hopes and his fears, for his living and his dying. Thou hast taught us through Christ to love our neighbor as ourselves: show us through him how large is thy concern for every deed we do for any of our brothers, whether building his house or selling him food, whether teaching his child or mowing his lawn. Spare us the shame of taking advantage of our brother in his need; keep us from making gods out of things, or things out of people; and as we use our special skills for those who use their special skills for us, let it be as if we laid them on an altar in an offering of praise to thee.

Thou didst create one world by the deed of thy

love. Thou hast made of one blood all of the peoples of earth. Empower us, we pray, to open the fists of hatred and extend the friendly hands of helpfulness. Still our angry passions; calm our greedy wills; and quiet every rising lust to claim for self some place of pride where others may not stand. Lead us to know at last the truth which thou must teach anew to every age and generation: that it is more blessed to give than to receive, that he finds his life first who first has lost it in the things of thy commanding, and that he loves thee best who best loves those for whom thou didst give the world thy Son, Jesus Christ, our Lord. *Amen.*

## *Reformation Day*

O thou God of all the ages and Father of all the children of men, who art no respecter of persons, neither holdest in awe the pomp and circumstance of man's creation, we praise thee that thou hast ever found a way to make thyself known to thy people. We thank thee for the gallant past that lies behind us, for the noble company of those who walked with thee of old and taught their children what they saw and heard, and more especially this day for thy servants the Reformers who braved the wrath of men to be the bearers of thy word. We speak our gratitude to thee for the Protestant churches and for their witness of thy power over sin and of thy will to meet thy people face to face.

There is no pride in us, O Lord, as we remember in shame that we have been many when we ought to have been one, that we have thought intolerance was faithfulness and vaunted bigotry as if it were an evidence of saintliness, that we have wasted our spiritual substance in petty jealousies and unfounded suspicions, and that in thought and word and deed we have not had in us the mind of Christ Jesus. Forgive, we beseech thee, that which we have been but ought not to have been, and that which we have failed to be but should have been. Sweep away our lethargy and selfishness. Renew in us awareness of our heritage. Confirm in us reliance on our hope. Keep us restless until we find our freedom in thy service, and grant that once again, as once of old, a Protestant shall be a witness-bearer, an apostle, a herald of thy power and thy love.

Yet it is for the Church universal that we pray in greatest earnestness, our Father: for the other congregations in this community and for every ministry of theirs that meets the test of thy truth, for all the churches of this nation and for each undertaking of their people that serves the common good of man, for the faithful hosts of every race and land and for the hope that from their faithfulness will come at last the day when all the families of thy folk shall be one family. Let thy church be filled with all truth in all peace, that the earth may resound with the joy of thy love and all who live have life everlasting. Through Jesus Christ our Lord. *Amen.*


*Thanksgiving*

Most gracious and most merciful God, thou who didst bring us to birth in a good land and cause us to dwell in the plentiful comfort of peace, thou who hast blessed us with bounty beyond all we either asked or deserved and surrounded us with love too wonderful for human understanding, we lift a common heart to thee and offer thee praise for every pure and perfect gift which thou hast urged upon us in this fair and lovely land. For the strength of this nation in food and shelter, for the freedom of its soil from war's devastation, for the faith of our fathers and the hope of our children, for the flicker of truth and the gleam of justice and the flame of compassion—we give thee humble thanks; for it is thou who hast made us and not we ourselves, and ever blessed by thee, we bless thee for thy blessing.

Yet even as we call to remembrance our cause for rejoicing, we heed as well, O Lord, our reasons for humiliation. No man lives who does not live because thou hast created him, but we have hated thy creatures whose skin is darker than our own, or whose noses are larger, or whose eyes are more slanting. Thou hast made man in thine own image, but we have treated people as if they were things and dealt with things as if they were people. We have preferred criticizing our neighbors to correcting ourselves, alleged the worst of motives in describing what our brother did and claimed the best in justifying the record of our own accomplishments, been jealous when we ought to have been generous and vengeful when we should have forgiven.

For these and all things else which we have done to bring thee pain, we ask thy pardon, our Father, and we pray that thou wilt so chasten our hearts that through the coming days we may learn to stand with those who stand with thee. Make us thankful for all the good that thou hast done in spite of all that man has done to thwart thee, and let not our gratitude be barren soil that bears no fruit in deeds of faith and love. Grant that our praise may rise from souls that have earned the right to praise thee. Draw us not back from the battles of thy purpose, and spare us no burdens that are big with thy will. For if we long to give thee thanks by giving thee praise, we hunger even more to do thee honor by doing thy will. Through Jesus Christ our Lord. *Amen.*

# PRAYERS
# AT THE OFFERING

Accept these gifts, O Lord, and let them be the tokens of our love and loyalty. May their ministry be holy in thy sight, and grant that those who use them in thy name may also use them in thy service. Through Jesus Christ our Lord. *Amen.*

We lift our offerings to thee, O God, and with them lift the lives whose fruits they are. Praising thee that thou hast taught us to give as freely as we have, we pray that thou wilt lead us into ever larger eagerness to share the burden of thy love; and wanting to serve thee now, we ask that thou wilt give us the will to serve thee with faithfulness far greater in the days that wait for us to live them. Through Jesus Christ our Lord. *Amen.*

Bringing these gifts in gladness to thy church, our Father, we bring them in even greater gladness to thyself. Receive them from our hands and hearts, we pray, and vouchsafe that through the power of thy love, they may be multiplied to thy glory. Through Jesus Christ our Lord. *Amen.*

O thou whose gifts to us are past all power that we have to give to thee, we have brought to thy house these tiny symbols of our gratitude and praise. Thy strength is made perfect in weakness, and through the insignificance of all that we can do for thee, we pray that thy might may loom the larger in the minds of thy children. Guide thou the use of these gifts, and so be in the hearts of those who are their stewards that they may magnify thy holy name. Through Jesus Christ our Lord. *Amen.*

O thou who lovest even those who have no love for thee, and who dost never set a price on thy goodness to thy creatures, we bring these gifts to thee in the fullness of our gratitude and praise. Transform our love for thee, we pray, until we love as thou hast first loved us, and giving, neither count the cost nor seek reward. Through Jesus Christ our Lord. *Amen.*

How can we give to thee, O Lord, who givest all to us? How can we bring thee any offerings which have not always been thine own? Yet, loving thee with grateful hearts, we return to thee this part of that which thou hast given us, and, committing it to thy glory, we pledge it to thy will. Through Jesus Christ our Lord. *Amen.*

We praise thee, O God. We glorify thee. We magnify thy holy name, and to the words that give our

*134*

adoration voice we add these offerings in the prayer that they may give it meaning for the world around us. Through Jesus Christ our Lord. *Amen.*

Receive these gifts of our hearts and our hands, our Father. Accept them as our testimony that we would serve thee with more than our words and that, having given because we love thee, we long so to love thee that we shall ever give thee more. Through Jesus Christ our Lord. *Amen.*

Where this portion of our treasure is, we pray, our Father, that our hearts may also be, and, offering thee our money, we pledge thee our lives. Through Jesus Christ our Lord. *Amen.*

We pray, our Father, that these offerings which we are about to make to thee may be acceptable in thy sight, and we ask that through the ministry to which we here commit them, thy will may be served in this church, in this community, in this nation, and in all those farther reaches of the world to which this church's hands can be outstretched in Christian love. Through Jesus Christ our Lord. *Amen.*

Receive thou these gifts, O Lord. Accept them for thy purposes, and teach us how to use them for thee in the service of thy will. Through Jesus Christ our Lord. *Amen.*

Because thou hast first loved us, we love thee, our Father; and because we love thee, we give thee back this portion of thine own, praying that thou wilt find pleasure in any warmth of sacrifice here represented, forgive any smallness of heart or tightness of hand, and so direct the use of these offerings that more is done by them than we could plan or hope. Through Jesus Christ our Lord. *Amen.*

Accept, O Lord, these offerings, which must often seem unacceptable to thy purity, thy glory, and thy majesty; and grant that through our sin thy holiness may be revealed, that through our smallness thy grandeur may be magnified, and that through our weakness thy strength may be made perfect. In Jesus' name. *Amen.*

Have pity, O Lord, on the smallness of heart which makes it so hard for us to open our hands to the needs of thy people. Spurn not the unworthiness of these gifts which we have brought to thy house, and grant that, remembering the love that sent the world thy Son, we may not withhold from thee the means of his ministry. *Amen.*

Forgive, our Father, the stain that lies upon these gifts we bring to thee. If we have earned them through dishonesty, if we have torn them from the hands of those to whom they rightly belong, if we have brought them to thine altar while the hurt we did our brother

still remains unhealed—forgive us and send us out at
the close of our worship with the will to right the wrongs
that we have done. Through Jesus Christ our Lord.
*Amen.*

O thou who art thyself a worker, bless the work by
which we gain the gifts we bring to thee. Let not the
hours spent in earning daily bread be hours spent apart
from thee, and, accepting our offerings, accept no less
the toil whose fruits they are. Through Jesus Christ our
Lord. *Amen.*

Almighty God, our heavenly Father, who callest
every man to be thy minister and to serve thee with the
special strength thou givest him, we dedicate our daily
labor to thy will; and laying on these plates this portion
of the money we have earned, we pledge to thy purposes
the toil that has produced it. Through Jesus Christ our
Lord. *Amen.*

God of creation and Father of men, because thou
hast not given us the special skills that missionaries need,
or ministers, or teachers; because we are too weak to
cross the seas and preach thy word afar or even serve
thee as we would in neighborhoods nearby; because
we lack the competence to heal a wounded heart or lift
a burdened soul or straighten minds that sin and guilt
have twisted—we bring our gifts to thy house that those
who can may do what we cannot. Help us, we pray, to
live anew in those who live in part through what we

give, and let the praise be thine forevermore. Through
Jesus Christ our Lord. *Amen.*

O thou who needest not the gifts of men since already thou hast all, we bring our offerings to thee in
part that they may minister for thee among our fellow
men, but in even larger part that we may share thy
mind and way, that we may learn the blessedness of
sacrifice, and that, giving what we have saved, we may
save what we have given. Help us, then, to gain with
gladness. Help us to give with rejoicing. Through Jesus
Christ our Lord. *Amen.*

Almighty and eternal God, who hast caused the
church to be the body of thy Son in the world, let these
gifts be hands and feet to him today. Let them be his
eyes to see the haunts of wretchedness and need, his
ears to hear the cries of loneliness and pain, his tongue
to call thy people to their proper service in thy name.
And grant to those by whom they will be used the
faithfulness to use them with wisdom and compassion.
Through Jesus Christ our Lord. *Amen.*

Separate our gifts from our sins, O Lord. Cleanse
them of any wrong that we have done in making them
ours, and, having purged them of their evil, take them
for thine own. Through Jesus Christ our Lord. *Amen.*

Almighty and eternal God, who hast humbled thyself to remain a spirit in a world where the fleshly wins

the quickest honors and who hast no hands but human ones to do the needed tasks of earth, we bring our gifts to thee that through their ministry thou canst again become incarnate; and we pray that thou wilt so cleanse the hearts of those whose task it will be to use them in thy name that, seeing their good works, men may give the glory unto thee. Through Jesus Christ our Lord. *Amen.*

Keep us humble in our giving, Lord. Spare us the folly of thinking that, having given what we do not need, we have given all that is needed. Keep us from hoping that we can so bribe thee with what we have that thou wilt not inquire what we are, and, leading us to give more freely, lead us at last to give ourselves. Through Jesus Christ our Lord. *Amen.*

So much of our treasure is buried, our Father— buried not like seeds that sprout and grow but buried like money hid in metal boxes and kept from all its destined uses. Thou hast said through Christ that where our treasure is, there, too, our hearts will be, and we pray that, bringing thee these little offerings which we have not yet buried, we may have the will to bring our larger treasures while our hearts are still alive. Through Jesus Christ our Lord. *Amen.*

The earth is thine, O Lord, the world and all the world contains; and lest we rob thee of thine own, we give thee back this part of that which thou hast loaned to us. Yet we would not rest content in such a trifling with thy majesty, and we pray that what we have kept for ourselves, we may use as those who have kept it for thee. Through Jesus Christ our Lord. *Amen.*

Thou hast given us so much, our Father, and we have given thee so little. Accept these offerings, we beseech thee, and grant that through the mysteries of thy providence they may be multiplied to thy glory. Through Jesus Christ our Lord. *Amen.*

Open our hearts and our hands to the needs of thy kingdom, O Lord, and let our gifts be the glad offerings of those who rejoice to do thy will. In Jesus' name. *Amen.*

# PRAYERS
# BEFORE
# THE SERMON

For him who speaks we ask the power to speak with truth and clarity, our Father; and in those who listen we pray for open minds and ready hearts. Through Jesus Christ our Lord. *Amen.*

Let that same mind be in us, our Father, which was in Christ Jesus our Lord. If we speak, may we speak the truth, and if we listen, may we listen with the will to understand and obey. In Jesus' name. *Amen.*

It is so easy, our Father, to mistake our words for thy Word. It is so tempting to put upon our prejudice the labels of thy Truth. Go before us in these moments, we beseech thee, and guard us lest we be false witnesses to thy will for this congregation. Through Jesus Christ our Lord. *Amen.*

Speak now to us, O Lord, through him who speaks for thee. Cleanse his mind of hidden error; purge his

*141*

heart of secret sin; and let his soul be so transparent in its openness to thee that thou canst shine through him upon a people eager for thy light. In Jesus' name. *Amen.*

O thou with whom alone all things are possible, we pray that thou wilt make thy strength perfect through the very imperfections which we now commit to thy glory. If thou canst cause even the wrath of men to praise thee, disdain not the halting mind or the stumbling word; and if thou canst not work thy will by means of us, win then thy victory in spite of us. Through Jesus Christ our Lord. *Amen.*

O thou whose Word is ever the same but who hast new words for every age and land, help us so to build our words upon the Word that none may speak nor any hear a word that is not thine. Through Jesus Christ our Lord. *Amen.*

Almighty and eternal God, who longest that thy Word be spoken and that, being spoken, it be heard and believed, we pray both for him who stands in the pulpit and for those who sit in the pews. Let not fear of man or thought of self corrupt the one, nor wandering minds and unruly affections lure the other. Through Jesus Christ our Lord. *Amen.*

Speak to us, O Lord, that we may speak for thee. Quiet our minds that though thy voice be still and

*142*

small, we yet may hear its thunder crashing in our ears; and vouchsafe that, speaking to those who listen or listening to him who speaks, we may rest content in nothing but thy Word. Through Jesus Christ our Lord. *Amen.*

Eternal Spirit, who art the source of all wisdom and knowledge, all goodness and love, help us to remember how easy it is to be mistaken—mistaken in our thinking, mistaken in our speaking, mistaken in our hearing. Keep us humble in these moments now before us. Give us open minds and ready hearts, and so chasten our wills that we do not substitute our prejudices for thy purpose. Through Jesus Christ our Lord. *Amen.*

Speak, Lord, for thy servants listen; and grant that when thy servant speaks, he may not forget that past all listeners he sees is One he does not see. Through Jesus Christ our Lord. *Amen.*

# PRAYERS

# AFTER

# THE SERMON

Forgive, O Lord, the weakness which has marred these moments now behind us—the ineptitudes of speech, the frailties of mind, the coldness of heart, the smallness of soul. Thou hast had a narrow channel for thy waters, and we praise thee for the patience which has not disdained to use it. In Jesus' name. *Amen.*

Our poor attempt to speak for thee is ended, Lord, and in thy care we leave the words that we have uttered. What we have said in truth, confirm. What we have said in error, correct. What we should have said but did not say, lead us so to live that we may see. Through Jesus Christ our Lord. *Amen.*

We have such little words with which to magnify thy name, our Father. Magnify our little words, we pray, that what we have so poorly said may not be said in vain. Through Jesus Christ our Lord. *Amen.*

O thou whose glory fills the heavens, what is man that thou dost regard him, or the son of man that thou dost think of him? We have tried to speak for thee, but we have known the while that we have seen through a glass darkly, known only in part, and heard like men whose ears were stopped against thy word. Discard, we pray, the trembling bridges we have sought to build between ourselves and thee. Span thyself the gulf that separates us from thy presence, and whisper in our hearts the truths which we have been too proud to understand. Through Jesus Christ our Lord. *Amen.*

. Almighty God, our heavenly Father, who knowest the hearts of us all, grant that the words which have been spoken here may reach their proper lodgment in our midst. Let not the lighthearted receive them too lightly, nor the overburdened find in them an added burden. Help us to remember from what we have heard the challenges that lie within our power to meet them, and vouchsafe that, having heard, we may heed. Through Jesus Christ our Lord. *Amen.*

Father of might and of mercy, in thy mercy forgive us our sins, and in our weakness sustain us with thy might. Prevent us from thinking that the words which we have heard exhaust the Word which thou wouldst speak to us, and keep us ever open to the truth that waits to claim us. Through Jesus Christ our Lord. *Amen.*

Forbid us, O Lord, the false comfort of making words a substitute for deeds. Let this sermon be for each of us not an end but a beginning, and as it falls behind us, grant that it may thrust us forward. Through Jesus Christ our Lord. *Amen.*

O thou who makest even the wrath of men to praise thee, use, too, the weakness and the error. Transform our whisperings to thunder, our candles to suns, our blunted pruning hooks to sharpened spears. What we have said in frailty, confirm with thy strength, and what we have heard with reluctance, teach us to heed with rejoicing. Through Jesus Christ our Lord. *Amen.*

Almighty and eternal God, who didst send thy Son to be the light of the world, grant that what we have heard, we may understand; that what we have understood, we may believe; and that what we have believed, we may do, until at last thy light so shines in our hearts that men see our good works and give the glory unto thee. Through Jesus Christ our Lord. *Amen.*

O thou whose gospel is always according to one of thy children, help us to realize how partial is the gospel according to ourselves. Let the words that we have heard be no more than windows on thy presence, and teach us to use them only as the means of going beyond them. Through Jesus Christ our Lord. *Amen.*

# PRAYERS
# AT THE CLOSE
# OF WORSHIP

Almighty God, who callest us both to worship and to work, our worship now is ended. Grant, we pray, that as we turn again to the tasks that lie before us, our work may not betray our worship, nor our worship loose its reins upon our work. Through Jesus Christ our Lord. *Amen.*

We have made so many noble resolutions, our Father. We have seen so many visions of the selves we ought to be, the hills we ought to climb, the deeds we ought to do. Go with us, we pray, as we enter the days that lie ahead, and grant that we may not prove false to what we have done in the hour that lies behind. Through Jesus Christ our Lord. *Amen.*

As we prepare to leave thy house, our Father, let it not be with the thought that we are leaving thee; and though our going be on separate ways, grant at last that all our ways be one. Keep us ever in the knowledge of thy presence; make our purpose always thine; and being apart awhile from one another, may we not forget the ties that bind us to our common Lord. In Jesus' name. *Amen.*

Send us forth in peace, O Lord, but not in complacency. Endow us with strength, but not with arrogance. Make us people of faith, but not of bigotry; people eager to love, but not to be meddlesome; people proud enough not to scorn themselves, but sufficiently humble not to be jealous of their neighbors. Through Jesus Christ our Lord. *Amen.*

If our minds have wandered from thee in this hour of worship, our Father; if our hearts have been cold; if we have considered more our fellows' wrongs than those which we have done ourselves; if we have come to this place to seek thy will but are preparing when we leave to follow our own: stay us in our homeward haste, we beseech thee. Restore our minds to consciousness of thee; warm our hearts in the closeness of thy love; save us from condemning ourselves in the judgments we pass on our brothers; and grant that in our bondage to thy purposes we find at last our perfect freedom. Through Jesus Christ our Lord. *Amen.*

We praise thee, O God, for thy ministry to us in this hour, and we give thee thanks for any word of thine which has won the welcome of our hearts. Let not the world reclaim us for itself, we pray, and in the waiting times of doubt and despair, in the coming days of weakness and temptation, grant that the memory of what we have been in these moments may return to strengthen and uphold. Through Jesus Christ our Lord. *Amen.*

Eternal Spirit, our heavenly Father, if we came to this house in the hope of thy blessing but think we leave it now with the hope unfulfilled, persuade us that we keep our doors awhile ajar. Save us from the rashness of hasty conclusions, and guard us lest thy judgment be that thou didst speak to those who would not listen, that we heard but would not heed, or that we sought a gift from thee which was not thine to give. Through Jesus Christ our Lord. *Amen.*

It is so easy for us to say that nothing happened, our Father, when the truth is only that we would not let it happen in ourselves. If we are about to leave thy house in the knowledge of some new blessing which thou hast here bestowed upon us, we thank thee. But if not, we thank thee none the less that the worship of this congregation has been the means of thy blessing for some of our fellows; and we pray that thou wilt lead us so to live in the week before us that, coming here again to praise thy name, we may stand at last among the surely blessed. Through Jesus Christ our Lord. *Amen.*

As we have praised thee with our lips, our Father, so now we would praise thee with our lives. In office or home, in schoolroom or store, in factory or open field—let all our words and deeds be offerings to thee, until we worship thee in work and, working, magnify thy holy name. Through Jesus Christ our Lord. *Amen.*

Weary we came to thy house, O Lord, and refreshed we turn away. Anxious, we have found peace; blind, we have seen light; weak, we have felt thine everlasting arms beneath us. For all that thou hast done in us we give thee thanks, and as we turn again toward home, we pray that we may not withhold our newfound strength from thee. Through Jesus Christ our Lord. *Amen.*

Let not the gap be large between the world of our worship and the world of our work, our Father, and grant that what we believe in the temple we may believe as surely in the marketplace. Save us from becoming split personalities, and if we spend our Sundays showing men that we are thy friends, guard us against using all our other days to prove ourselves thy foes. Through Jesus Christ our Lord. *Amen.*

We praise thee, O God, for the heritage out of which our worship has come. We thank thee for the Christian centuries which lie behind us and which both sustain our faith today and thrust us toward a greater

*152*

day not yet disclosed to us. Keep us from being only spectators of the church's history, only passengers for the Christian voyage, only parasites upon the martyrs' sacrifice; and grant that, resting on the faith of our fathers, we may not rest too long. Through Jesus Christ our Lord. *Amen.*

# PRAYERS
# FOR THE SACRAMENTS
# AND ORDINANCES

## BAPTISM

### (*Child*)

Father of might and of mercy, who hast ordained that life begin in helplessness and love be found in sacrifice, hear us, we pray, as we receive this child into the family of thy people, and guard us lest we ever lay a stumbling block across his path. Illumine our minds that we may guide him in wisdom; warm our hearts that we may lead him in love; and purify our souls that we may not withhold from him the gift of faith in Jesus Christ. *Amen.*

### (*Adult*)

O thou who art the sovereign of the worlds and the master of the ages, the giver of life and the lord of all living, we stand in awe before the mystery of thy providence, and we praise thee that thou hast laid thine hand upon this man who is now to be admitted to the company of thy servants. We speak the words, we make the proclamations; but only thou canst know the heart, or cleanse the soul, or lead the self beyond its selfishness. Grant then that the deeds done in this hour may be outward signs of invisible graces. Let the voices of men be the voice of thy will and the door of thy church be the gate to thy kingdom. Through Jesus Christ our Lord. *Amen.*

## (*Child*)

God of all power and love, the life and light of men, we praise thee for the miracle of birth and for the wonder of the minds and hearts, the souls and bodies, which thou dost daily bring to being on the earth. We bless thee that thou art a workman of infinite resourcefulness and patience, that no creature of thine is but a copy of another creature, and that thou givest the world new hope whenever thou givest thy people a child.

Especially we thank thee for this child who has here been acknowledged thy son. Let the deed which we have done in thy name be an act performed to thy glory, and grant that through the years that lie ahead the pledges made in faith may be fulfilled with unswerving devotion. Bless thou this child with health, our Father, but bless him even more with holiness. Lead him to respect himself but not vaunt himself, to be just but not unmerciful and merciful but not unjust, to seek thy kingdom first but not to think that he can stand long in thy presence unless his brother stands beside him. Empower his parents so to live that he may not find their precepts more desirable than their example. Fill their home with patient wisdom and enduring affection, with broad sympathies and noble purposes, with reverent faith and humble readiness to serve their fellows in their need. Kindle in thy church an eager concern for the home here represented, and in the fellowship of those who love thee, let the home be so sustained and surrounded that this little one may be numbered at last among the loyal followers of Jesus Christ, having no fear save fear of thee, loving only that which thou dost find lovable, and claiming no reward except the benediction of thy favor. In Jesus' name. *Amen.*

### (*Adult*)

Almighty and eternal God, who hast never left an age without a witness to thy glory nor kept a people from the knowledge of thy will, we gather here to praise thee for the unspeakable gift of faith by which thou hast set this man apart to thy service. We thank thee for thy great goodness in the revelation of thyself to him, and, receiving him into thy church, we pray that thou wilt so confirm him in his promise of discipleship that the years may find him steadfast and the record prove him true.

Come to him in this hour. Come to him and make him wholly thine. Thou hast called him to love thee with all of his mind, and we ask that he may not disdain the sturdy disciplines of Christian scholarship; but save him, we beseech thee, from becoming no more than an intellectual machine, a repository of facts, a cold storage vault that has no windows on the far horizons of mystery and the bright blue skies of thy grace. Thou hast called him to love thee with all of his heart, and we ask that his comradeship with thee may ever have the warmth of those who love and do not count the cost; but save him, we beseech thee, from speed without direction, from intensity without tolerance, from fires that do not drive pistons but only blow up boilers. Thou hast called him to love thee with all of his soul, and we ask that thou wilt sometimes lead him into breathless hours when thou dost dwell with him alone; but save him, we beseech thee, from assuming that he can love thee without loving his neighbors. Thou hast called him to love thee with all of his strength, and we ask that thou wilt have no patience with laziness in him, with cowardice, self-pity, or lack of compassion; but save him, we beseech thee, from the blindness that sees in life no power other than its own, that has no faith in anything except itself, and that has lost awareness that the Creator of the universe is capable of sustaining his creation.

Keep thy servant proud enough to be earnest and humble enough to be teachable. Protect him alike from parading his faith on street corners and from hiding his light behind the darkened lenses of fear. Teach him so to lose his life that his loss will be gain and that, being thine, he will be most surely himself. Through Jesus Christ our Lord. *Amen.*

## THE LORD'S SUPPER

Almighty God, who dost daily die that we may daily live, we call to remembrance the death of thy Son, and, acknowledging our many offenses against thy love, we confess that he endured the cross for our sake. Forgive us, we beseech thee, and prepare us so to eat the bread and drink the cup that, kneeling in shame, we may rise new creatures in thy sight. Through Jesus Christ our Lord. *Amen.*

Thou hast often spoken to us in word, our Father: speak now in deeds. Let the bread be broken, let the cup be emptied; and, heeding again the Master's commandment, may we feel once more his presence among us. Forgive us. Cleanse us. Save us. In Jesus' name. *Amen.*

Holy Spirit, who speakest in silence with a word that is louder than thunder, let these quiet moments be a voice for thy will. Show us in the bread the body broken, and in the cup reveal to us again the blood that was shed for our sins. Let no heart come to thy table hungry and turn away unfed, nor any soul approach the sacred place in arrogance and leave it without the humbling of his pride. Through Jesus Christ our Lord. *Amen.*

Heavenly Father, who art the King of kings and Lord of lords, but who still didst love the world enough to send it thy Son, we gather again at his table, and again we do the deed that he commanded. Guard us, we beseech thee, lest we eat the bread lightly or take the cup not knowing what we do; for as we touch again the sacred symbols, we would not forget the One who gave them.

That night in the long-ago days of Herod the King when Joseph and Mary appeared before the inn at Bethlehem of Judea, the Wise Men from afar, the shepherds on the hills, and the little boy born among the animals of the stable because there was no room for him in the inn—we would remember Jesus. The humble family in the house behind the carpenter's shop on a narrow street of Nazareth, the widowed mother and the many mouths to be fed by him who was the oldest of the children of Mary, the romps on the hills by day and the long, long dreams beneath the stars of Galilee's nights—we would remember Jesus. The baptism by John in the River Jordan, the forty days of lonely strife in the wilderness, the calling of Peter and the other disciples, the Sermon on the Mount and the lessons by the way, the healing of the halt and the ill—we would remember Jesus. The last days in Jerusalem, the sweat that fell like blood in Gethsemane's garden, the death on the cross, and the empty tomb

where men had thought that death was king forever—
we would remember Jesus.

Yet we pray that thou wilt so open our hearts to
him that his coming may be more than a memory. Let
his living presence be among us, and as we dwell a while
with him, let that same mind be in us which was also in
him. Help us to be just and not to fear the conse-
quence. Help us to be generous and not to count the
cost. Help us to love and not to fear that we are being
foolish. Teach us to deny ourselves, to take up our
crosses, to love our enemies, do good to those who
hate us, and pray for those who despitefully use us.
For we ask not that we be ministered unto but that we
have the will to minister, not that Christ belong to us
but that we belong to him. *Amen.*

Almighty and most merciful God, who dost reveal
thyself to the humble and withhold thy presence from
the proud, we assemble at the table of thy Son, and
we seek the confidence of those who feel thee near. We
read the words of Scripture, written of old by men
who saw thee not as far away; we sing the sacred
songs; we lift up our voices in prayer; we receive the
sacrament of faith delivered to our hands by those
who walked the earth before us; and ever we ask that
on the roads we strive to build toward thee, thou wilt
find a way to come to us and be known of us forevermore.

Thou understandest how we long for some clear
sign both *that* thou art and *what* thou art, but thou

understandest, too, how, longing for thee, we hold thee off, because we fear to meet thee face to face. Give us then that humbleness of spirit without which none can truly be brave. Give us that courage without which any sight of self cannot endure to see the whole of self. Give us that awareness of our creaturehood without which pride puts out the very eyes that search for thy footsteps.

Once more let the bread be broken before us, Lord; again let the cup be poured out; and grant that, remembering the Master's death for our sake, we may comprehend thy will for man. Create in us the heart to see aright what things are great and what things small, what ends deserve our sacrifice and what other goals, though prized on earth, are still no more than folly in thy sight. Save us from selling our souls for a larger home, a newer automobile, a bigger bank account, or a higher standing in the social circles. Vouchsafe that we may have the grace to live the life which, being most truly simple, is most surely profound, and which, most surely denying the self, most truly gives the self fulfillment. Increase the days when thou dost back us out of harness, when thou dost teach us how to rest and how to wait; and in the meeting of our daily problems remind us often that the Word made flesh still dwells among us and that the day is yet unknown when thou art not the Lord.

We come to thee together and alone, our Father, and both one by one and as a congregation of thy people, we eat the bread and drink the cup, pledging ourselves that he who did not scorn the cross shall not be scorned by those whom he died to redeem. Confirm us in that will, we beseech thee, and deliver us from the evil that so speedily ensnares us, lest being thy friends, we serve thy foes. Through Jesus Christ our Lord. *Amen.*

# ORDINATION

Father almighty, who callest men to ministries of many kinds, we praise thee for the deed which thou hast done in this man set apart for thy service. As he makes before his fellows the pledges long since made to thee, confirm thy will in him, we pray, and grant that those who now surround him with their love may sustain him with their faithfulness. Renew in all of us the eagerness to be thy ministers, and let the people of this church so become thy people that they glorify thy holy name. Through Jesus Christ our Lord. *Amen.*

O thou Holy Spirit, against whose coming man cannot defend nor from whose going save, we thank thee that thou hast come to this servant of thine in whose name thy people here have gathered, and we pray that thou wilt never have the need to leave him. So guide us in this hour when he takes upon himself the duties of thy kingdom that they who speak may speak thy truth, that those who hear may hear thy Word, and that every thought and aspiration may be found acceptable to thee. Out of worship lead us back to labor, and, having ordained thy servant to his sacred ministry, may we neither ordain him to our own forgetfulness of him nor, having faith, be found unfaithful. Through Jesus Christ our Lord. *Amen.*

Almighty and eternal God, who hast summoned men to speak for thee in every land and age, we gather in this holy place to celebrate anew the stirring of thy Spirit in the hearts of thy people. We thank thee for thy gift of Jesus Christ and for the light which he has shed upon the darkened ways of earth. We thank thee for the men of old who, becoming thy disciples, became apostles, too, and thus the means whereby we learned of Christ ourselves. And now we give thee special thanks that in thy providence a call has come to him who kneels before these symbols of thy love and sacrifice.

Accept the offering of life he makes to thee, we pray, and by thy might so cleanse and guide and strengthen him that the sacred pledges of this day may be incarnate in the time to come. Make him a preacher of thy Word, O Lord, and bestow upon him both the boldness of a man who knows that he knows thee and the humbleness of one who knows that he knows thee only in part. Make him a pastor of thy people, Lord, and grant that while he speaks thy truth without distortion, he may share thy love without restraint. Make him a workman holding rightful place among the other workmen of thy kingdom, Lord, and as he strives to know and do thy will for himself, vouchsafe that he may also lead the men and women of his charges so to know and do thy will for them that he and they together may be priests of thine and avenues of grace between the world of spirit and the world of flesh.

Setting him apart for special ministry, we pray that he may never be apart from thee or from the ones whom thou wilt place within the province of his care; and as we lay our hands upon him now, we ask of thee that thou wilt make these hands the instruments of thy purpose. Do thou for him what men can never do. Stand him on rock. Free him from fear. Fill him with goodness. And through the days and nights of earthly life chasten him in thy justice, purge him by thy purity, support him with thy power, and direct him through thy wisdom, until when death shall end at last his ministry on earth, thou canst welcome him to further fields without regret and receive into thy joy a good and faithful servant who has not departed from thy way.

All this we pray in the name of Jesus Christ our Lord, and to thee be the power and the glory, world without end. *Amen.*

Almighty and eternal God, who in every age hast summoned men to speak thy Word and do thy will, we praise thee for the glory of thy being and for the richness of thy love. Knowing thee only in part, we thank thee for what we have known, and, understanding how far our ignorance exceeds our knowledge, we thank thee even more for the vast reaches of thy providence which stretch beyond our comprehension. Because we have fallen short of that which thou didst intend us to be, we ask thy forgiveness; and because we long so much that day may dawn where only night has been, we turn with special earnestness toward this man here set apart to serve thee in the fullness of his Christian ministry. We hold him up to thee, and we pray for him as if he were thine only child.

Grant, our Father, that he may be brave, but not so brave that he is foolish. Grant that he may be humble, but not so humble that he has no pride in thee and in the heritage of those who kept the faith before him. Being just, may he also be merciful; and being merciful, may he not forget thine everlasting righteousness. Give him peace, but not the peace of those who never see the agony which they could spare their fellows, and give him restlessness, but not the restlessness of those whose hope has small horizons. Keep him from the atrophy of a mind which, never being used, is never usable. Save him from the condemnation that, having little love for thee, he had great love for thy gifts; that, blinded by his people's sins, he never saw his own; and that, living in a day of tumult, he did not share its pain.

Let not the fire lie unkindled in this soul, O Lord. Denying thy servant the arrogance of those who think that thou hast cared for them more than their fellows, leave him not either in the thought that thou hast cared for him less. Create in him the magnetism of a great

*166*

enthusiasm. Reveal to him both the strength he has and the weakness, and then so guide him day by day that his strength is found upon thine altars and his weakness made the instrument of wider sympathy with all thy heavy-burdened children.

As we lay our hands upon him, we pray that thou wilt receive him into the company of thy faithful apostles and that thou wilt empower him to be a preacher whose words speak only thy Word, a pastor whose love is as thine own, a teacher whose stores of truth are gladly opened to his people's need, and a priest who knows that he cannot long find welcome in thy presence unless his brothers be with him. We speak our gratitude to thee for this holy moment in which the years of preparation are laid before thy throne as the offering of a life to be gained by its loss, and for the days that lie ahead we ask no more for this man than that for which we know we have no need to ask—the same full measure of thy love which thou dost always give to men in Jesus Christ our Lord. *Amen.*

## MARRIAGE

Almighty and everlasting God, beneath whose eye man's life is lived and from whose love all earthly loves arise, hear this man and woman as they make their solemn pledge of faith to thee and to each other. Let not the skies of earth confine this deed we do with them, and vouchsafe that the words we speak have warrant in thy Word, that the union we celebrate meet approval in thy sight, and that the promises here made be never broken. Through Jesus Christ our Lord. *Amen.*

Eternal Father, who dost kindle in thy children the love for one another, we praise thy name that thou hast engendered in this man and woman the will to be united in marriage and to seek thy blessing on the home that they establish. Touch their hearts in this hour, we pray, and let that mind be in them which was also in Christ Jesus. Confirm them in their high resolves for the life that they will live together, and empower them so to pledge their faith to each other that they may ever keep with faithfulness their promises to thee. In Jesus' name. *Amen.*

Eternal and merciful Father, who alone canst unite the hearts of thy children in love, join this man and woman, we beseech thee, in that love which man can neither give nor take away. Grant them patience through the early years when life must fall in step with life, when love is often both most wonderful and most wonderfully difficult. Save them from exaggerating each other's faults and minimizing their own. Save them from words spoken in anger, from grudges nurtured in silence, and from callousness before each other's needs. Save them from the waning of reverence, the dimming of wonder, and the cooling of affection.

Before they were lovers, they were friends, O Lord, and we pray that the coming of love may not mean the departure of friendship. Respecting themselves, may they never lose respect for one another, and, bound to one another, may they ever be more surely themselves. Surround their home with wide horizons; deny them peace in worldly comforts; lift their eyes to roads of service; and as the busy days sweep on around them, let not embarrassment or self-indulgence thwart thy claim on their discipleship.

To thy tender care we here commit them. In health and in sickness, in abundance and in want, in life and in death, abide with them that they may not withdraw from thee. Through Jesus Christ our Lord. *Amen.*

Almighty and eternal God, who hast ordained that thy people dwell in families and who art ever present when a man and woman join their hearts as one, we praise thee for the providence which has stirred the love of each other in the hearts of these thy servants. Be with them as they here acknowledge thy lordship over them, and empower them to make their home a dwelling place for thee.

Grant that their love may be patient and kind, not jealous or boastful, not arrogant or rude. Save them from insisting on their own way; defend them from being irritable or resentful; and vouchsafe that, rejoicing, they may ever rejoice not at wrong but in the right. Let their love bear all things and, bearing all things, believe all things. Let it hope all things and, hoping all things, endure all things.

Thou knowest all things, our Father, and thou

169

knowest how readily the gray monotony of time can dull an early rapture, how speedily the intimacies of a home can become the instruments of evil. Guard this man and woman from ever taking each other for granted; from ever being tyrannical or obsequious or hateful; from ever using the other as the means to an end. Shield them from unfaithfulness in deed, but steel them, too, against disloyalty in thought and word. Teach them how much of love is the free gift of thy hand and how much grows only on the trees of loving-kindness. Sharing each other's joys, may they share as willingly their sorrows. Blessed by each other's strength, may they not disdain each other's weakness. Needing to be forgiven, may they not withhold their own forgiveness. For we pray that thy kingdom may come in them, thy will be done in them. Through Jesus Christ our Lord. *Amen.*

## FUNERAL

O thou holy Spirit, whose years cannot be numbered, nor whose power thwarted, nor whose love encompassed, we praise thee for the word of everlasting life which has come to us in Jesus Christ, and we glorify thy name for every intimation that when the dead have died in thee, they are not dead. Dwell now among us in the loss of one whom we have cherished. Let the memory of him be blessed in our midst, and vouchsafe that, sustained by faith in life eternal, we may find in death a way to life. Through Jesus Christ our Lord. *Amen.*

Eternal God, who knowest both the ages and the moments and who carest alike for the one and the many, we call to thy remembrance a well-beloved soul whose earthly life is ended. From work and play we gather here to celebrate the good that we have found in him, and commending him to thy powerful mercy, we pray that thou wilt confirm in us the hope and love that we have seen in him. For his sake lead us to be faithful and in his name to bear the burdens thou hast taken from his hands. Through Jesus Christ our Lord. *Amen.*

God of all power and love, who canst do what is best for thy children and who carest enough for them to do what thou canst, we praise thee for thy great goodness in the life of this man whom we have lost from our sight. The years slip through our minds like minutes when we think of him, and, remembering the days that we have had with him, we thank thee for the providence that let us call him friend. For his devotion to thee and his service to thy church, for his integrity in personal relationships and his faithfulness in the surging flood of daily duties, for his steadfast courage, his stubborn righteousness, and his compassionate concern for the oppressed and disinherited—we hold his name in honored place among us and pledge to him our loyalty in days to come.

There is sadness in our hearts that he cannot be with us now as once he was of old, when his body was strong, and his way was clear, and life seemed fair and fine; but in our hearts, too, there is the kindling joy of those who see his course on earth guided at last to thy long-destined ending and lifted from the growing menace of the twilight into the gleaming dawn of a whole new world beyond our present understanding. Watching him depart a while from us, we give him not to death but to thee, who, being Lord of life, art Lord of death as well. We do not fear for him, nor think of him as wandering alone in lands of pain and fear. Instead, we look toward days when heart shall welcome heart again, and comradeship be made as never broken, and all eternity be seen to stretch ahead for fellowship with thee. And when in time to come the thought of him steals into mind once more, grant that we may see him marching onward still as he was wont to do on earth—eyes ever forward, heart always alert, and soul in constant restiveness before the threat of helplessness or inactivity.

We would that he might still be with us on the earth, our Father, but not if he could not be healthy. We would that he might still be with us on the earth, our Father, but not if he could not be happy. We would that he might still be with us on the earth, our Father, but not if he could not be free to do the things he loved to do and walk the ways he loved to walk. So we give him back to thee who gavest him to us, and we give thee, too, the praise and the glory, world without end. *Amen.*

Holy and eternal God, who art too merciful to be weak and too mighty to be cruel, age after age the living seek thee, and in thy sight the generations rise and pass away. Yet thou knowest them one by one. Thou callest them by name, and thou carest for each as if thou hadst no care for any child save him alone. They pass from us but not from thee; they depart from the earth but not from thy love; and though the mountains dissolve and the seas disappear, though the sun be destroyed and the earth vanish, thy watchful eye is on thy creatures, and thine everlasting arms are round about them.

For all the blessed dead we give thee thanks, and especially for this man raised to remembrance before thee. That we could know him, that we could be the benefactors of his graciousness and wisdom, that there were times when we could share his burdens or smooth his road or ease his pain—these thoughts are precious to us, Lord, and as the body's senses lose their grip upon him, we pray that thou wilt be to him as a lamp for his feet and a light for his way. And if it be that he has knowledge of the life we live without him, let him have no doubt that we have not forgotten him, that his memory is dear among us, and that we hold in eager hope the day when we shall see him once again as face to face.

Vouchsafe as well, our Father, that we may prove our faith through faithfulness and demonstrate our love by lovingkindness. Keep us from supposing that valor was more cheaply bought in other days than now. Protect us from assuming that the pain and sacrifice of ancestors were borne more easily than ours would be today. Save us from believing that because we had a noble antecedent, we ourselves are noble; and spare us the error that because the past has blessed us with a goodly heritage, we must deserve it more than those less favored. Make the past a blessing to us that we in turn may be a blessing to the days yet to come. Lead us to discontent that we should be no more than parasites, and allow us no peace until we make our own full contribution to the life of man on earth. Guard us lest we eat the sour grapes of evil and set our children's teeth on edge; fill us with love of thy law; and on all the unknown roads ahead, so guide our feet and our hands, our minds and our hearts, our wills and our souls, that in the end thy kingdom may come and thy will be done among us. Through Jesus Christ our Lord. *Amen.*